The Principles of
TEACHING RIDING

The Principles of

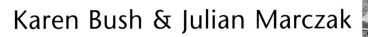

Karen Bush & Julian Marczak

TEACHING RIDING

The Official Manual of
the Association of British
Riding Schools

David and Charles

With especial thanks and gratitude to those teachers
who have been a constant source of encouragement and
inspiration for me and countless other pupils:
Christine Carter BHSAI, Alison Midwinter BHSI,
Daniel Pevsner FBHS, and Charles Harris FIH FABRS FBHS.

Karen Bush

I have been fortunate indeed to have had excellent teachers,
namely my mother, Suzanne Marczak, also Charles Harris,
Phillipe Davenport and the late Maestro Nuno Oliveira. All, in
their different ways, I have regarded as first-class horsemen in
the true classical tradition, and
I wish to acknowledge their help and encouragement with
warm thanks. Above all I dedicate this book to my mother,
who against all odds has toiled endlessly to build
Suzanne's Riding School into the establishment it is today.

Julian Marczak

Authors' Note

Throughout this book, he, his, and him have been used as
neutral pronouns and are intended to refer to both sexes.
Where the word 'horse' is mentioned, it includes mares,
geldings and ponies, but not stallions.

The authors would like to thank the following for
their input and comments whilst reading through the
manuscript during preparation of this book:
Shirley Renowden FABRS;
Charles Harris FIH FABRS FBHS;
Lt Col (Retd) Gordon Wesley FABRS, BHS(SMT),
ABRS Prin Dip, NSBD

Photography by Kit Houghton

(except pp47 & 107 Bob Langrish)
Artworks by Maggie Raynor

A DAVID & CHARLES BOOK
David & Charles is a subsidiary of F+W (UK) Ltd., an F+W
Publications Inc. company

First published in the UK in 2001
First UK paperback edition 2005

A catalogue record for this book is available
from the British Library.

ISBN 0 7153 1095 X hardback
ISBN 0 7153 1902 7 paperback

Book design by Visual Image
and printed in China by RR Donnelley
for David & Charles
Brunel House Newton Abbot Devon

Visit our website at www.davidandcharles.co.uk

David & Charles books are available from all good bookshops;
alternatively you can contact our Orderline on 0870 9908222
or write to us at FREEPOST EX2 110, D&C Direct, Newton
Abbot, TQ12 4ZZ (no stamp required UK mainland).

Foreword

Teaching riding is one of the most enjoyable and rewarding aspects of association with the horse or pony. Whilst expecting a teacher to have patience and foresight, and the ability to maintain discipline, he must also be able to understand, communicate with, and win the confidence of, each and every pupil.

It is the teacher or trainer's role to give both pleasure and satisfaction, and good instruction breeds good habits in the rider and produces disciplined, obedient horses and ponies. If the teacher is also a true animal lover then care of the horse or pony's needs will be guaranteed and true understanding of the animal's mind achieved.

The greatest satisfaction of all comes from the sharing of continued progress and improvement with the rider. *The Principles of Teaching Riding* gives due attention to all these aspects of horse, rider, and teacher relationships and I recommend it as a necessary addition to your equestrian library.

Pauline Harris FABRS
Chairman of the Association of British Riding Schools

Contents

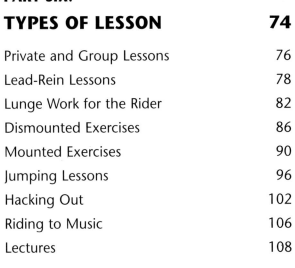

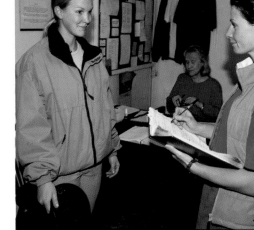

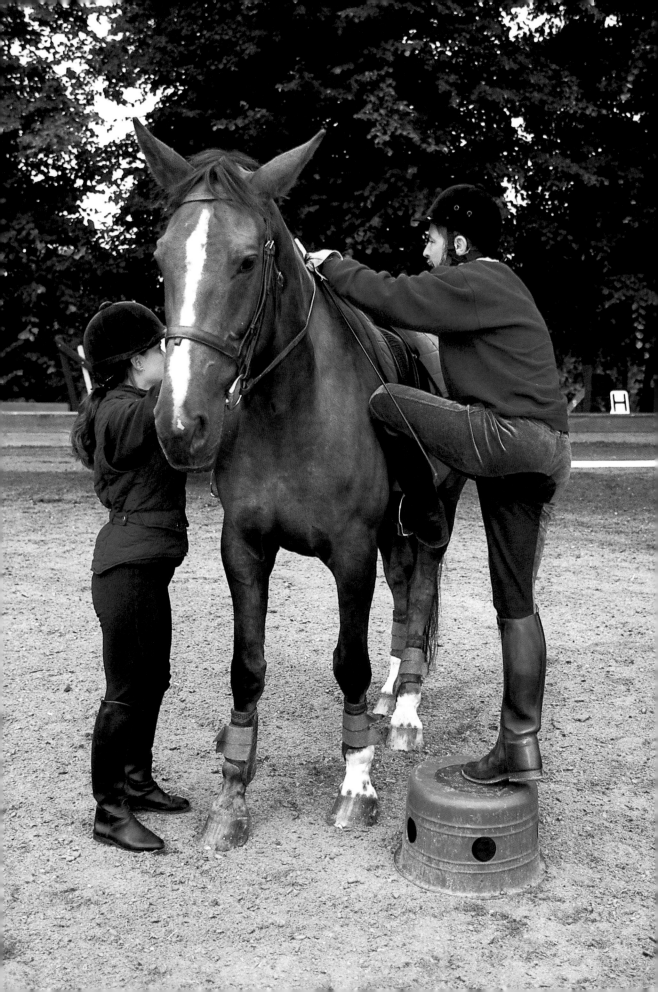

Introduction

To the best of my knowledge, *The Principles of Teaching Riding* deals with a subject which has never before been fully explored and/or properly undertaken on a sound professional basis.

The joint authors offer a comprehensive and unique approach to the basic and primary elements upon which all first-class riding instruction depends, and how these principles should be applied, so that teacher and pupil, irrespective of age and experience, are governed and protected by the professional care – and safety – expected when attending an Approved riding establishment.

The Principles of Teaching Riding spells out in simple, clear and concise language the essential material factors and practicalities concerned in teaching horse riding. Examiners of horse riding teachers/instructors the world over should be presented with a copy of this publication by their respective associations and societies, which I believe would raise their own standards of riding instruction and, even more importantly, improve the standards of riding safety on and off the riding establishment. This work has been presented in such a way that adult beginner riders – and the parents of child beginner riders – will also find it of immense value as it details correct and safe procedures which should be carried out from the moment beginner riders (and others) enter the riding establishment.

Due to the book's scope and coverage this publication is recommended not only to the principals and their teaching staff, but for everyone taking part in any form of equestrian activity in commercial riding establishments. Simply and expertly written, *The Principles of Teaching Riding* is an important encyclopaedia of principles and precepts which should be looked upon as the 'bible' for the safety of horse and rider, and is highly recommended.

Charles Harris FIH FABRS FBHS

PART ONE:

Fundamentals

The Horse

✔ A good school horse is a valuable asset.

✔ Care should be taken to ensure that more popular horses do not become overworked.

Horses and ponies provided for the use of pupils in the riding school must be as suitable and safe for the purposes of giving instruction as reasonable skill and care can ensure.

Age

It is illegal for horses or ponies below the age of four years to be used for tuition in riding establishments. Realistically, it may be found that some animals are unsuitable for instructional purposes at this minimum age, as they may lack schooling and be insufficiently mature mentally and physically to cope with the demands of commercial riding-school work.

Conformation

The conformation of the riding-school horse should be as correct as possible to ensure that it moves correctly and is capable of carrying the rider safely. A horse which is well put together is also more likely to remain sound during the course of its working life.

It is illegal for any horse which is unsound to be used in a riding establishment; neither should those which are in poor or obese bodily condition, or in need of shoeing be used, for reasons of rider safety and out of consideration for the horse.

Temperament

A kind temperament and generous nature are also essential attributes for riding-school horses, and where these are not present, it is likely that the horse will not be suitable for the

purposes of riding-school work. It should also be noted that horses or ponies which have some known propensity for potentially dangerous behaviour such as biting or bucking, or which may be unpredictable or unreliable in their behaviour, are not suitable for riding-school work; moreover, if they are used, and an injury to a rider does occur, this may result in a successful claim for damages being awarded against the establishment.

Variety

A variety of horses of different heights and builds will be necessary if a wide range of pupils is to be catered for. When calculating weight-carrying ability it should be borne in mind that height alone does not offer an accurate guide when matching horses to pupils, but conformation and density of bone must also be considered.

The sex of the horse is largely immaterial, although teachers should be aware of the fact that some mares may exhibit a degree of irritability and touchiness when in season, and they should be vigilant for signs of this, exercising care in the management of lessons on such occasions. Stallions should not be used in riding schools.

Schooling

Even a horse with good conformation may move poorly or adopt undesirable evasions if it is lacking in schooling, has been badly trained, or is subject to frequent use on lessons involving inexperienced riders. Horses used for riders receiving instruction must be sufficiently well schooled and

A variety of different heights and builds of horse will enable a wide range of pupils to be catered for

Too large a horse (left) or too small a horse (right) will inevitably cause problems for a pupil and could lead to poor posture, insecurity, lack of control and possibly accidents. An overlarge rider may also adversely affect the balance of the horse and cause considerable discomfort to it

obedient that the tuition given will be constructive, and the lesson safely accomplished.

Regular schooling by capable members of staff will help to ensure that the horse retains a correct, supple and obedient way of working. Furthermore, teachers should try to ride each horse at least once a month in order to make a practical assessment of its qualities and/or limitations; this will help to prevent unreasonable demands being made of either horse or pupil.

Fitness

Horses and ponies must be fit enough to cope without distress with the work they are required to do. It can be easy for more popular horses to be over-used, so that they become excessively tired and soured by the workload, and this may result in faulty locomotion and/or possibly dangerous evasions which may affect the safety of the pupil. It should be appreciated that although riding-school work is generally steady in nature, it can nevertheless be demanding on the horse. As a suggested guideline, each horse should not work for more than a maximum of two hours in succession without a break, and with a maximum of four to five hours per day depending on the type of work involved. Where a horse is required to undertake a more physically demanding and intensive lesson – for example, private jumping instruction – he should be allowed sufficient recovery time afterwards, and his daily workload should be reduced accordingly.

Teachers should show consideration for the welfare of the horses at all times during lessons, allowing frequent periods of rest, particularly for older horses. These may be in the form of individual exercises being ridden whilst the remainder of the ride walks, or of the entire ride either walking on a long rein or halting during discussion of exercises and movements. Weather temperature will dictate whether horses stand still or keep moving during these periods.

The teacher should also strive to make his lessons as varied and interesting for the horse as for his pupil.

Suitability for the rider

It is the responsibility of the teacher to ensure that each pupil is allocated a horse or pony which is suitable and safe for that individual, taking into account the pupil's age, height, weight, experience, riding ability and any known handicap or limitation. Failure to take these factors into account may mean that the pupil has difficulty in adopting a correct posture and that he encounters control problems, and accidents are then more likely to occur.

SAVING THE HORSE

Pupils should be encouraged to make use of mounting blocks where available. When using a mounting block the teacher should additionally support the opposite stirrup to prevent the saddle from slipping.

Giving a leg up is another way of avoiding placing undue strain on the horse's back when mounting.

The Teacher

✔ When a rider is experiencing difficulty, the teacher should be experienced and imaginative enough to understand the nature of the problem and be able to 'talk' him through it step by step.

✔ The teacher's most difficult task is not so much in teaching the pupil how to use his seat, back, hands and legs, but in teaching him to think for himself and to apply correctly what he has been taught.

The riding teacher is many things to many people: more than merely a repository of knowledge, he must be prepared to act as coach, guide, adviser, mentor, lecturer, disciplinarian and commanding officer. In addition he needs to be something of a politician, psychologist and psychiatrist, and on occasion may also find himself cast in the role of first-aider, trusted confidant and friend.

Qualities

The required qualities of a good teacher are numerous, but essentially he must possess the following characteristics:

- Constant vigilance for the wellbeing of his pupils. The teacher is responsible not just for ensuring that his pupils enjoy and gain benefit from lessons, but also for their safety, and he should therefore strive to ensure that accidents do not occur as a result of his negligence, carelessness, or poor and unsafe teaching practices.
- Infinite patience, particularly with slower learners.
- Impartiality to all pupils, favouring all equally and not singling out any for special attention.
- Being trustworthy enough not to relate to others any confidences disclosed to him by his pupils.
- Sensitivity to the particular needs and requirements of individual pupils and horses; and possessing an intuitive feel for when to ask more, and when pupil and horse have achieved as much as they are able at that time.
- Being alert to recognise when a horse is tiring of being asked to perform a particular movement, or is simply becoming fatigued; and/or when the rider is in a similar state. Also he must be able to appreciate when a particular act is beyond the capacity of horse or rider.
- Honesty without tactlessness: he should extend civility, diplomacy and courtesy towards his pupils, treating them with respect and as equals.
- He should be imaginative enough to adapt his teaching methods and strategies to the individual requirements of pupils and horses, and relate to their difficulties. He should be able to see when something is not working, and to find a different, more successful approach.
- An open-minded attitude, constantly seeking to refresh/refine/extend his own knowledge, both to his own benefit and advancement, and that of his pupils.
- He should always be approachable to all who seek his advice and help.
- The ability to employ common sense and logic to resolve difficulties.
- A genuine desire to promote the cause of safe, sound equestrianism and to pass on his enthusiasm to others.
- Excellent communication skills.
- Horsemanship skills sufficient to be able to demonstrate correctly to his pupils the principles he espouses, or to effect improvement in a difficult horse when necessary; also for the purposes of assessment.
- The ability to set a good example to his pupils, and to be a good advertisement for the riding establishment.
- Being confident and secure enough in himself to know when he has taken a pupil as far as he is able; and to suggest the pupil seek tuition from another teacher.

The Rider

✔ More pupils ride purely for pleasure than for serious competition.

✔ Unlearning is far more difficult than learning. Be patient with those who have much to undo.

✔ Clients who do not derive enjoyment as well as improvement from lessons are unlikely to return for many more.

Each pupil approaches riding with differing ambitions: some may wish only to become proficient enough to be able to enjoy hacking out, whilst others will view it as a pleasant way of taking physical exercise, and a social occasion as much as an educational experience. Still others may have – or may develop during the course of tuition – a more serious interest in equitation, a desire to train for exams or professional qualifications, or perhaps to work towards competitions.

Whatever their personal ambitions or level of competence, all pupils have in common the right to expect the following from their lessons:

- The teacher will take every care to ensure their safety.
- The teacher will treat them at all times with respect, consideration and courtesy.
- The tuition they receive is stimulating, constructive, enjoyable and based on sound, correct classical principles.

Aptitude

Pupils can vary widely in natural aptitude, intelligence, build and physical ability, and the teacher should take all of these factors into account, tailoring his tuition accordingly. He must take care not to ask the pupil to do anything which is beyond his capacity to produce at the time of asking, as such failures will be disheartening, may dissuade him from making further effort, or even to discontinue his riding activities altogether – and can lead to accidents.

However limited a pupil may seem initially, or however humble his personal ambitions, the teacher should never be condescending, nor underestimate a pupil's determination to succeed – indeed, he should give him every encouragement and help so that he does succeed.

New pupils

New clients should be briefed on the procedure of paying for, and booking further lessons; they should also be informed as to yard safety, and to policy with regard to cancellation fees. In addition they should be asked to fill in a confidential registration form providing their address and contact telephone numbers, plus any relevant information regarding previous riding experience, also details of their height and weight, and any medical/physical problems. Clients should be requested to inform staff of any changes in these details so that the information can be kept up to date.

A system by which pupils may be graded ensures that they can be placed in a group lesson most suited to their abilities, with other riders of a similar standard

GRADING OF RIDERS A grading system of some description has benefits for both staff and pupils:

- It helps ensure that pupils do not feel 'miscast' by being placed in a lesson with other riders who are either less able, or more skilful. This can lead to embarrassment, loss of confidence, possible accidents, and general discontent which may cause them to take their custom elsewhere.
- It can instil in pupils a sense of achievement and satisfaction at having reached a certain standard of competence, and helps stimulate a desire to progress further.
- It assists staff in determining the abilities of a new pupil, so that a suitable horse or pony can be allocated.

Either an internal form of grading, ABRS Equitation and Stable Management Tests, or other recognised qualifications can be used instead of, or to further subdivide the broad groupings given opposite. Where an internal system of grading is employed, the criteria which need to be met at each level should be documented and kept readily available for staff to consult.

Pupils can be divided broadly into four categories:

■ **Beginner**: A pupil who knows little or nothing about horses and ponies, and who should receive instruction in a safe, enclosed school or outdoor arena.

■ **Novice**: A pupil who can manage a quiet, obedient horse or pony in walk, trot and canter, and is able to jump small obstacles up to 18in (45cm) in height within an enclosed school or outdoor arena. He is also sufficiently competent to go out for a hack.

■ **Intermediate**: A pupil able to tack up, mount and take an obedient horse or pony into the school, to ride with confidence in all gaits and transitions, always maintaining full control, and to jump a variety of small obstacles up to approximately 30in (75cm) in height and spread, including simple gymnastic grid exercises; he is also quite capable of going out on hacks. On returning to the stable yard, he will be able to remove the tack, and to rug up the horse or pony.

■ **Advanced**: A pupil capable of producing some lateral work, of jumping fences in excess of 30in (75cm) in height and spread, and of competing in small local shows. He also has a good knowledge of correct stable management and horse care procedures.

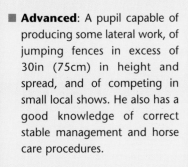

The Rider

Assessment of new pupils

Some pupils may over-exaggerate when asked to describe their abilities. For this reason, all new pupils should always be given an assessment lesson in order to determine how well – or not! – they ride, and thus the most appropriate lesson for them to join. This also applies to those riders who may have no desire to participate in formal riding instruction on a regular basis, but wish merely to hack out. Under no circumstances must a rider be allowed to leave a riding establishment mounted until he has first demonstrated his competence to ride in walk, trot and canter. Such assessment lessons should take place within a safe, enclosed area and on a steady, sensible horse or pony, and in the instance of a client interested only in hacking, a competent escort should be allocated to him on the first two or three rides out to further assess his ability.

Lesson progression

Occasionally the teacher may come under pressure from an ambitious pupil to transfer him to a more advanced group lesson. Whilst remaining courteous, if the teacher feels that the pupil is not yet ready for such a move, he must be prepared to resist this and explain the reasons. These are usually in the interests of safety and the pupil's correct development and progress. In such instances, having a definite grading system in operation, and one which stipulates the specific skills to be achieved at each level, can be helpful in keeping over-ambitiousness in check, whilst causing the minimum of offence.

Safety

In order to minimise the likelihood of an accident occurring, all clients, regardless of their level of ability, should never be allowed – or asked – to ride or handle horses and ponies either within the riding establishment or out on hacks except when under supervision by a competent and experienced member of staff.

Insurance companies as a rule will not grant public liability insurance to riding establishments which allow riders to ride unaccompanied by an experienced and/or qualified person appointed by the establishment, and this should be borne closely in mind. Likewise, where public liability insurance has been granted, it may well be deemed invalid in the event of an accident occurring where the rider has not been under supervision in this way.

Do not assume that because a new pupil has done something before, he knows how to do it correctly. Check that he can lead his horse safely to and from the school, holding the reins in the right hand behind the horse's jaw and keeping the other end in his left hand, not trailing them along the ground. He should walk beside the horse, remaining between its eye and shoulder, on its near (left) side. The stirrup irons should be run up leathers at all times except when the pupil is either preparing to mount or is mounted.

The Riding School

✔ Greet clients in a friendly fashion on their arrival: don't leave them to wander round on their own feeling lost and unwelcome.

✔ An untidy, dirty yard is dangerous, and does little to inspire confidence in prospective clients.

✔ Public relations should be included as part of staff and student training – at the end of the day it is the client who pays the wages.

The environment in which pupils are taught should be conducive to making the tuition they receive safe, constructive and enjoyable. Riding schools vary widely in the facilities they are able to offer, but basic provisions for the benefit of clients must be made, and these should include:

■ good parking facilities;
■ a clean reception area;
■ a safely enclosed arena or indoor school;
■ an office;
■ separate male and female toilets with washing facilities;

■ safety helmets for hire, which conform to current safety standards;
■ a first-aid box containing items that are maintained at current safety standards.

Additional facilities might include a reception area with seating and tea/coffee-making equipment, and changing/wash rooms: although optional, these are often greatly appreciated by clients and will do much to make the time they spend at the establishment before and after their lesson, more pleasant and enjoyable.

(Left) All tools should be kept tidily and safely stored when not in use

(Far right) Yards should be kept tidy, both for safety and to ensure a good impression

Safety on the yard

The riding-school environment should be made as safe as possible for all concerned – horses, clients, vsitors and parents alike. A Health & Safety Policy should be written indicating how the proprietor manages safety within his establishment in accordance with one of his statutory obligations, this being compliant with the Health & Safety at Work Act 1974. Guidance leaflets are available from HMSO on this subject.

Proprietors and staff should pay especial attention to the following points:

- Stabling and ancilliary buildings should be soundly constructed from safe materials, and kept in a state of good repair.
- All electrical wiring should be in good order, with no trailing or loose cables, and wires and switches sealed. Circuit breakers should be installed where necessary.
- The yard should be adequately lit when in use after dark.
- All tools should be put away after use. Ideally they should be hung up on racks with adjacent notices displayed, stating 'All tools should be hung up after use with sharp edges turned inwards'.
- Other items such as bales of hay and straw or buckets should not be left lying around where they might pose a hazard to movement around the yard.
- Potholes, uneven paving and broken steps can also be dangerous, and in icy conditions measures should be taken to help prevent slipping.
- A stringent non-smoking policy on and around the yard should be observed.
- All veterinary medications, wormers, rodenticides etc. should be safely and securely stored.

SIGNS/NOTICES Signs should be displayed to ensure that clients can find their way around without difficulty, particularly in larger yards – these might indicate where facilities such as the school, tackroom, office, toilets and so on are to be found, as well as those areas which are off-limits to the general public. There should also be names or numbers on stable doors so pupils can easily and correctly identify the mount they have been allocated. A noticeboard situated in or near the booking/reception area, with details of prices and any planned events or activities, is helpful too.

Signs and safety notices should be prominently displayed; these should include:

- Safety policy notice. The ABRS can provide a specimen notice to member schools upon request.
- A noticeboard displaying the public liability insurance certificate, a copy of the riding-school licence issued by the local authority, and certificates of the teaching/first-aid qualifications held by staff.
- 'No Smoking' signs.
- The location of fire extinguishers and buckets.
- A fire point, with clear instructions on what action should be taken in the event of fire.
- The location of the telephone.
- The location of the first-aid facilities.

PART TWO: Facilities

& Equipment

The Riding Arena

✔ Teachers should not instruct from horseback, or from the viewing gallery, where one is present. Ride control and the ability to act quickly in emergency situations is best effected from the centre of the school.

✔ The teacher should try to ensure the minimum of external disturbance whilst lessons are in progress: this is particularly important for novice and nervous riders.

✔ Overhead electrical cables, lighting and sprinkler systems must allow adequate head clearance for riders working over fences as well as on the flat.

Suitable facilities must be available in which to teach. An indoor school, or a well constructed, drained and fenced outdoor all-weather surface can provide an ideal safe environment for pupils, and in addition ensures that lessons can continue throughout all, or most, of the year.

Surface maintenance

A wide variety of different materials are available for arena surfaces, but all will require regular maintenance and attention to some degree if they are to fulfill their function of providing a level surface with good going which will reduce the risk of injury to the horse's limbs, and enable him to work safely, easily and correctly. Some materials will require topping up at intervals, and/or watering to reduce dust to the minimum. Material which builds up against the retaining boards should be levelled regularly – as indeed should the whole surface – either by raking by hand, or by using a pony or small tractor pulling purpose-made equipment for this job. Some surfaces may also need occasional harrowing to keep them loose, re-mixing with specialist rotavating equipment, or rolling: the manufacturer or supplier will be able to provide more detailed information concerning these aspects.

Maintenance should not be neglected: it need not be overly time-consuming if conducted on a regular basis, and it will extend the working life of the surface, improve its efficiency, and ensure that the whole area can be safely utilised.

VIEWING AREA/GALLERY A viewing area or enclosed gallery is not essential but it does allow clients, visitors and parents to watch lessons in safety and relative comfort. Any windows facing the riding area should be higher than the top of the kicking boards or enclosing fence, and if glazed, toughened, non-reflective glass should be used.

The use of cones to help mark out school figures such as circles will encourage accurate riding

Enclosure

The riding arena should be fully enclosed by fencing of suitable, sturdy construction that stands at a minimum height of 4ft 6in (1.4m). In indoor arenas, brick walls should be lined with wooden kicking boards or sleepers to a similar height, and angled outwards from the base at a slope of 12–15° from the vertical. Walls of indoor schools should also be of a light colouring.

Entrance doors should be a minimum of 10ft (3m) in height and 8ft (2.4m) in width, and should either slide sideways or open outwards. A sign with instructions detailing the correct procedure for entering or leaving the school should be displayed on, or near to, entrances and exits.

(Left) Wear on those areas of the school which tend to receive particularly hard usage, such as the outer track, can be reduced by using poles to create an inner zone within which horses can be ridden

LIGHTING   Lighting is required for evening lessons and when teaching indoors on dull days. This should be efficient: too few or underpowered lights will cast areas of the school into shadow, making it difficult for the teacher to observe his pupils, and may be responsible for some horses exhibiting a degree of spookiness in certain places.

Switches for lights should be situated in a safe position and easily accessible to the teacher, as he may wish to turn the lighting on during the course of a lesson, and must be able to do so without leaving his pupils unsupervised.

Dimensions

Teaching groups of pupils requires sufficient space if horses and riders are to remain safe and not become too bunched up, and to permit a variety of school movements to be ridden. Dimensions similar to that of a standard-size dressage arena, measuring 66 x 132ft (20 x 40m) are suggested, as this allows scope for both flatwork and jumping lessons. Areas in excess of this may create difficulties for novice pupils still learning to control their mounts.

When teaching group lessons of children with small ponies, it may be helpful to further reduce the size of the arena by a third or even a half, by using portable lightweight hurdles, so that individual exercises do not take excessively long for each rider to complete. A smaller area will also make it easier for the instructor to safely control the entire group.

Layout of a 20 x 40m arena (right) and a 20 x 60m arena (far right)

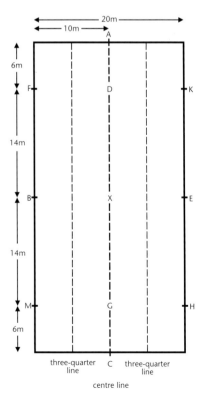

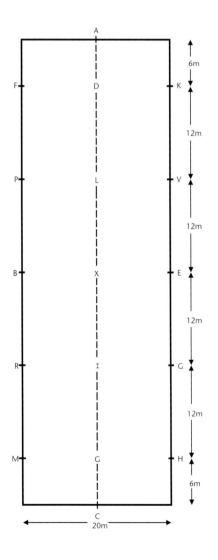

Rules of the School

1

2

For their own safety as well as that of others, all new pupils should have the 'rules' of the school explained to them during their first lesson.

Entering the school (1)

Anyone wishing to bring a horse into the school must first ask permission to do so from the teacher currently inside, even if the lesson is no longer in progress. Only when permission has been given should the horse be led in, and the door or gate closed securely behind him.

In the school (2)

On entering the school, the horse should be brought into a safe position – generally on the centre line unless specifically instructed to move elsewhere – where he can stand whilst the saddlery is checked, adjusted, and the rider mounts.

When groups of riders enter the school, they should all line up together at a safe distance from each other to avoid any danger of kicking and biting between horses.

Passing other riders (3)

When overtaking another rider moving in the same direction on the outside track, warn him in advance of the manouevre, and pass by on his inside (that side of the horse closest to the centre of the school), giving him plenty of space.

3

Right of way (4)

When passing another rider moving in the opposite direction, always pass left shoulder to left shoulder. Those on the outside track on the left rein (anti-clockwise direction) therefore always have right of way over those on the right rein (clockwise direction) *except* if the rider on the right rein is:

- moving in a faster gait; or
- is engaged in lateral work: if both riders are in lateral work, then the one on the left rein has the right of way.

Similarly, riders moving in faster gaits have right of way on the track over others moving in the same direction in slower gaits: and those in lateral work have right of way over others moving in the same direction on two tracks, regardless of their gait speed.

Gaining right of way

If a rider has right of way on the outside track, and finds that another horse is blocking his way he should call out loudly and clearly 'Track free' to warn of his presence, and his intention to continue along it. Such warnings must be given sufficiently in advance as to enable the other rider to move out of the way.

Passing other riders (5)

When passing other riders, plenty of room should be allowed between each horse to avoid any incidence of kicking or biting, and to ensure that the one closest to the wall does not feel trapped, causing him to panic.

Leaving the school (6)

Riders should ask permission when they wish to leave the school, from the teacher instructing at the time. Until permission is given, the horse should be positioned in a safe place on the centre line, away from the exit.

✔ Doors and gates should be well maintained so that they are easy to open and shut.

✔ When horses are in the arena or indoor school, doors and gates should always remain closed, except when a pupil is entering or leaving with the permission of the teacher.

Riding Outdoors

✔ Lessons must never be conducted in fields where grazing animals are present.

✔ If animals are to graze the area used for riding when it is not in use, all equipment must be cleared away to prevent injuries and damage.

More advanced pupils who have attained reasonable control of their horse in all three gaits may enjoy the opportunity to ride on grass when the weather and ground is suitable. At riding centres which enjoy more extensive facilities, this may also include the opportunity for tuition over varied terrain as preparation for supervised hacking, or for cross-country and show-jumping instruction.

Ground

Areas used for flatwork lessons should be level, well drained, and situated away from overhanging tree branches or potentially dangerous fencing such as barbed wire, ditches or electric fencing. Rough, tussocky patches of grass will not be conducive to good schoolwork and should be trimmed back to avoid any danger of the horse stumbling.

A suitably sized area to work in for flatwork lessons can be marked out using portable dressage boards, poles, cones or Bloks, and letter markers set out at the appropriate points to encourage accurate work.

Jumping lessons

As with flatwork lessons, fences used for jumping lessons should be sited on an area of level, well drained ground away from hazards such as overhanging tree branches, ditches and fencing.

Permanent cross-country fences must be correctly and sturdily built. Simpler options at a variety of heights should be included, as well as more complex ones involving ditches, water and undulating terrain. Before attempting these the teacher must be confident that the pupil has sufficient skill and control of his horse, and has been properly briefed on the appropriate way to tackle them.

Weather conditions

The teacher should always take into account the effect of weather conditions on the horses as well as the ground, and plan lessons accordingly, if necessary being prepared to move them to a more predictable and safer environment with better going. For example, high winds may cause some horses to become anxious or spooky, whilst a previous spell of wet weather or even just a brief shower of rain may cause grass to become treacherously slippery.

In dry weather the ground can rapidly become baked hard, and horses worked excessively on it, particularly if jumping, may begin to suffer from the effects of concussion, and possibly incur lameness.

PRECAUTIONS   Some horses may become very excitable when first introduced to work out in a field, particularly if they are used to spending most of their time in an enclosed riding arena. Therefore, with the onset of better weather each year, before regular lessons outdoors commence, each horse should first be worked in the environment by experienced and competent members of staff in order for him to become accustomed to it.

Riding outdoors, whether on an all-weather surface or on grass can make a pleasant change from the confines of an indoor school for horse, rider and teacher

Arena Equipment

✔ Leave your own problems at home so you can give your full attention to those of your pupil.

✔ Be prepared to demonstrate a new movement by riding or walking through it for pupils: it may be that your verbal communication was unclear.

✔ Never allow pupils to jump fillers without a pole resting on them. If a horse or rider were to brush against one it could cause a nasty injury.

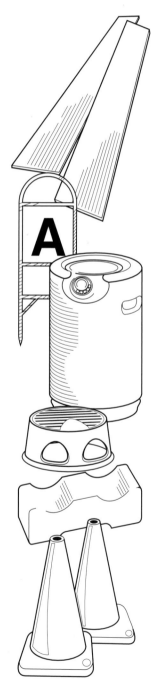

In addition to a suitable riding area(s), a selection of equipment will be helpful to both instructor and pupil for school exerccises and jumping instruction.

Markers

Letter markers should be correctly positioned and permanently fixed around the school to enable the teacher to give clear and precise instructions to the pupil for riding turns, circles and other school movements; this will also help the pupil to learn to ride with accuracy. The markers will also help pupils who are working towards dressage competitions to become familiar with the layout of a dressage arena.

If younger children are taught, the letter markers may be accompanied by a picture of a familiar animal or object, the first letter of which corresponds to the marker it is positioned beside – for example, a picture of an apple next to the 'A' marker. This can add an element of fun and informality to the lesson, and it avoids difficulties if the child is dyslexic or unfamiliar with the alphabet.

Additional markers: Other markers indicating the three-quarter line are also useful teaching aids: these can be simply added by marking the wall or fence on each short side with white paint at the appropriate points.

Portable markers: When flatwork lessons are taken out in a field, the riding area can be defined with portable dressage boards or coloured show-jump poles, and portable letter markers placed around the edges. Purpose-made letter markers may be bought, or the letters may be painted onto 'Bloks', or plastic cones or drums.

Cones: A set of twelve plastic cones (similar to those used at roadworks), 'Bloks' (see page 32), or drums are another useful aid when teaching pupils to ride school figures and movements accurately. 'Bloks' also make easily movable mounting blocks. Metal drums should not be used as they may injure the horse if it brushes against one. Plastic drums should be weighted by partially filling them with sand or water so they cannot be blown over by gusts of wind.

MIRRORS Although not essential, suitably framed mirrors can be an invaluable aid to pupils in checking their position and straightness, and when executing lateral work. They should be made of toughened glass, and be mounted securely at a height of not less than 6ft (1.8m) and tilted at a slight angle so that they may be used from the opposite side of the school.

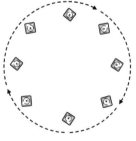

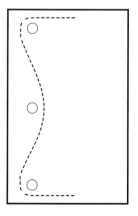

Jumping equipment

Further equipment will be needed in order to conduct polework and jumping lessons: this need not be extensive or costly, but it must be safe and correctly used.

Poles: Poles should be smooth, rounded, with a minimum diameter of 3½in (9cm) and 10–12ft (3–3.5m) in length. It is preferable if they are a uniform length as this will cause fewer problems when constructing fences. Avoid very heavy poles: they are awkward to lift and the horse may injure or frighten itself if it knocks one down. Rustic poles should not be combined with coloured ones in single obstacles or grids of ground poles because they are inclined to blend into the background colour of the working area surface and so are less easily visible.

Wings and jump stands: Wings or jump stands need to be reasonably lightweight but without being flimsy, so they can be moved around quickly and easily with less risk of the instructor suffering back injury. Jump wings, where used, should be full rather than half size; this will create a more inviting fence, and allow more sizeable obstacles to be built for advanced pupils.

'Bloks': 'Bloks' are a useful alternative to jump wings: made of moulded plastic, they are lightweight, easy to move, allow a variety of obstacles to be built, do away with the need for jump cups, and can be used as markers for figure riding. They are also extremely strong and durable, and will not rot if they have to be stored outside; neither do they need repainting, nor require a large amount of storage space. They should not be used with gates and planks as the recesses are for rounded poles.

Other accessories

In addition to poles, well equipped riding centres may possess obstacles such as planks, gates, fillers and walls. When incorporated into an obstacle, free-standing fillers should always form the lowest element, with one or more poles or planks which can be dislodged, suspended above from the appropriate type of cups. When wooden walls are used, either a pole should be hung above it in like manner, or a row of light wooden coping bricks laid along the top.

STORAGE OF EQUIPMENT   Equipment should always be put away tidily after use: a storage area should be designated for this, outside the riding arena, but close enough to allow easy and convenient access to it when required. Leaving equipment within the school, even if neatly stacked, is highly inadvisable and dangerous. Always put away jumps which are not in use.

PLASTIC DRUMS

Drums should never be used either as wings to support poles or planks, or beneath them as fillers, as they can be extremely dangerous if the horse hits the jump. The only circumstances in which they may be employed acceptably and safely, is if they are fixed in such a way as to be immovable – as part of a permanent cross-country fence, for example – or if they are cut in half lengthways and used as fillers, when they will be quite stable. For safety reasons only plastic drums should be used, never metal.

Far left (from top): portable dressage boards, letter marker, portable markers, 'Bloks' and cones. These provide suitable markers for exercises in the school (left), help the teacher to give clear instructions and, in the case of the letters and boards, allow pupils to become familiar with the layout of a dressage arena

---

Jump cups should be shallow rather than deep, so that poles resting on them can be quite easily dislodged if they are hit by the horse. Rounded cups should only be used for rounded poles, never for planks, gates or hanging fillers: flat cups must be used for these so that they fall easily if knocked.

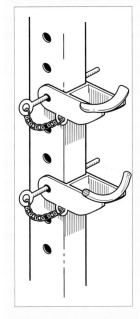

Integral cups and pins, or cups where the pins are attached with a short length of chain, are ideal, as the pins will not become separated and lost, or accidentally left lying in the riding area where they could injure a horse should he step on one.

PART THREE: Horse &

Rider Equipment

Saddlery

✔ Be prepared to be open-minded and to modify your ideas, but do not seize eagerly at each new idea of equitation or item of equipment that you hear about until you have tested it for yourself and discovered if it is safe and has any worth or practical application.

✔ A good teacher presents facts in an organised way.

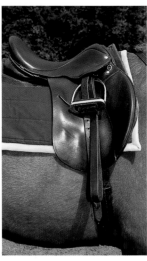

A GP saddle (left) suitable for jumping, hacking, or for flatwork with a novice rider, and (right) a dressage saddle appropriate for a more advanced pupil working on the flat. As well as type, the saddle should be of an appropriate size for the rider

Correctly fitted snaffle bridle (left), and (right) fitted with the noseband too high and the bit too low. It is essential for the welfare and comfort of the horse that all saddlery is correctly fitted, as well as to ensure that the rider can control him safely

All saddlery used during the course of a lesson must fit the horse correctly: if it is ill-fitting, not only may it result in injury to the horse, but the discomfort it causes can lead to unreliable behaviour such as bucking, rearing, napping or kicking, that could be dangerous to the horse and rider, and to others present.

Ill-fitting or badly adjusted saddlery will affect a rider's ability to control the horse, and compromise safety.

The saddle

The saddle must be suitable for the level of rider and the type of activity: thus a dressage saddle would not be appropriate for an inexperienced pupil, for hacking, or for jumping lessons.

Not only should the saddle be a good fit for the horse, but it must also be large enough to accommodate the rider so that he is able to adopt and maintain a correct and safe posture at all times whilst mounted.

The bridle

As with the saddle, bridlework must be a good fit, and not cause pinching, chafing or any restriction of the horse's breathing. Reins should be of a suitable length: if excessively long the pupil's feet may become caught in them, whilst if too short he will be unable to maintain a correct posture and contact with the horse's mouth.

The bit is commonly of a snaffle type with a smooth mouthpiece: horses which require more severe bitting than this (or various martingales and other auxiliaries to the bit) are unlikely to be suitable for the purposes of normal riding-school work. The exception to this is when teaching a pupil on his own

SAFETY AND MAINTENANCE A member of staff should be nominated to be responsible for undertaking regular saddlery inspections, and for ensuring that repairs or replacements are made as necessary. In addition, all items of saddlery should be cleaned daily to prolong their working life and to keep them supple and safe; at the same time they should be checked, as a matter of course, for signs of wear and tear.

Tack correctly fitted with horse moving freely on a loose rein

horse, or advanced horses and pupils during flatwork lessons when a double bridle may be deemed appropriate.

Neckstraps

The provision of a neckstrap on each horse is a sensible idea, benefiting both horse and rider; it is certainly to be recommended for beginners and all jumping lessons.

Stirrup irons

Stirrup irons must be of adequate width for the pupil's feet. If they are too narrow his feet may become tightly wedged in them; too wide, and they might slip right through and become trapped: in both instances the rider's balance will be affected, and there is a risk that he may be dragged by the horse in the event of a fall. The use of rubber treads is advisable to help prevent the pupil's feet from slipping on the metal of the irons.

INCORRECT

INCORRECT

Stirrup leathers

Stirrup leathers should be long enough for tall pupils, but with a sufficient number of holes that they can be adjusted to suit shorter people: they should never be twisted around the irons to shorten them as this damages the leather and causes the irons to hang at an incorrect angle.

Pupils should be taught how to correctly and safely check and adjust the length of stirrups and girth tightness, before and after mounting. The rider should keep a correct rein contact and both feet in the stirrups while mounted. Teachers should always check that saddlery is correctly adjusted and fitted before allowing riders to move off

Stirrups which are adjusted so as to be too long (left) or too short (right) will create security, communication and balance problems for the rider, as well as giving rise to discomfort and distorted posture

Saddlery

PRE-LESSON CHECKS   Regardless of routine
checks made by staff, or the competence of the riders, the
teacher should always check for himself the saddlery of his
pupil's mounts before each lesson commences, and satisfy
himself as to the correct fit, adjustment and safe
conditions of all items. Any saddlery which fails to meet
these requirements should be adjusted or replaced
immediately before the horse and pupil are allowed to
continue. Never put the safety or welfare of horse or rider
at risk through neglect of this aspect, even though it may
result in lessons running late. Salient points to watch out
for include:

- weak and/or missing stitching;
- areas of leather which have become stretched, worn
  and thin; buckle holes running into each other; twisted
  buckles or which have shortened or bent tongues;
- numnahs, if used, should be pulled up into the front
  arch and gullet of the saddle;
- saddle correctly positioned;
- girth lying flat, not twisted, attached to the correct
  girth straps on both sides, and sufficiently tight both
  before and after mounting;
- throatlash not overtight; also the browband, which
  should not pull the bridle headpiece forward into the
  base of the horse's ears;
- noseband at the correct height, not fastened outside or
  twisted around the bridle cheekpieces, and tightened
  appropriately according to its type;
- bit at the correct height and lying evenly across the
  horse's mouth;
- reins not crossed beneath the horse's neck;
- both stirrup leathers lying flat against the rider's legs,
  and adjusted so as to be of equal length;
- the thumbpieces on the stirrup bars should be lying in
  the 'down', not the 'up' position.

Stable management

Injury and discomfort to horses may be caused not only
through the use of ill-fitting saddlery, but by neglect of
good stable management practices. After lessons, sweat
marks beneath the saddle, girth and bridle may be
washed off if the weather is warm enough to do so without danger of the horse becoming chilled; or allowed to
dry before being thoroughly brushed off. Failure to do
this, or to ensure that the horse's coat is free of mud and
dirt before tacking him up, can quickly lead to galling
and sores.

Saddlery should be regularly cleaned to prolong its life and ensure that it does not cause chafing or galling. This is also an ideal opportunity to check for any areas which require repair

Clothing

✔ Any rider wishing to remove a jacket or jumper during the course of a lesson should, after getting permission, dismount first rather than attempting to do so whilst still in the saddle.

✔ Pupils preparing for a competition may need to be advised on the correct dress and saddlery for that particular discipline – information on this can be found in the relevant rule books. As rulings are subject to changes from time to time, ensure that any literature you consult is up to date.

Whether taking part in a lesson, or going out on a hack, pupils need to be suitably dressed for riding in order to be both comfortable and safe. Beginners should be briefed on appropriate garments to wear when booking their first lesson, and no pupil – of any level – who is unacceptably dressed should be allowed to ride.

Clothing which causes discomfort or restricts movement will interfere with the pupil's ability to adopt and maintain a correct position in the saddle. Correctly fitted specialist riding clothes avoid these problems as well as looking smart, but they can be expensive to purchase, and novice riders may understandably be reluctant to spend much money on such items until they are sure they are going to wish to continue with their riding activities. In such instances compromises can be made, but as soon as possible pupils should be encouraged to equip themselves in more correct attire, and in particular to invest in a riding hat which meets current safety standards.

Legwear

Jodhpurs are ideal, provided they are not excessively tight; a more casual alternative are the stretch jeans especially designed for riding. For beginner riders, stretch leggings are acceptable in the short term. Ordinary denim jeans, stretch or otherwise, are not suitable because they have heavy seams on the inner leg which can chafe painfully against the inside of the knee and crotch.

Footwear

Safe footwear is vital: full-length riding boots or jodhpur boots are best, but other alternatives are acceptable, provided they are sturdy, flat-soled and with a heel of not less than ½in (13mm) or more than 1in (25mm).

Wedge or platform heels, heavily ridged soles, Wellington boots, trainers (other than the type designed specifically for riding which have a heel), sandals and shoes with buckles are all potentially dangerous: they generally offer little protection to the toes if these are trodden on by the horse, and they may cause the feet to slip through, or out of, or to become wedged in the stirrup irons.

Jackets

During wet or cold weather, it is sensible for the pupil to wear warm, weatherproof clothing: this should, however, be as close-fitting as possible to avoid any danger of it becoming snagged up on anything, and to enable the teacher to observe the rider's upper body position. Lighter, thinner layers of clothing and thermal underwear is preferable to very thick jumpers and padded jackets which may impede mobility. When jackets are worn they should always be fastened at the front, so they do not flap around and frighten the horse, or interfere with the pupil's movements.

Formal dress (left) is appropriate for examinations, competing or when judging at shows, but more casual clothes (far left) are perfectly acceptable for lessons, when teaching and for everyday riding, provided they are safe

The teacher should make an effort to dress correctly and tidily, as a mark of courtesy to the pupil, to set a good example, and to enable him to ride when necessary for the purposes of assessment, demonstration or correction. He should on no account mount a horse unless he is wearing correctly adjusted and secured protective headgear conforming to current safety standards, and also suitable footwear.

In examination situations dress tends towards the formal, but during everyday riding and teaching activities it is generally more practical and comfortable to adopt correct casual clothing. This is perfectly acceptable provided it is safe, functional and smart.

Body protector

Hats

All pupils *must* wear correctly fitted and secured protective headgear when mounted, and which conforms to current safety standards. These standards change from time to time: if you are unsure as to current specifications, the ABRS can be contacted for advice.

Some riding centres and schools may keep a supply of riding hats available for hire by new clients, and which should also meet current safety standards: any which are damaged or suspected to have sustained damage in a fall should be discarded and replaced.

Attention should be paid to ensuring a correct fit when hiring out hats, checking that it is a snug but comfortable fit, worn squarely on the head and with the retaining harness properly adjusted. Some manufacturers run hat-fitting courses, when staff may be trained in this aspect. No pupil, at any time, should be allowed to ride with the retaining harness undone.

Underwear

Underwear is a topic which some pupils may be too bashful to inquire openly about, but if it is ill-fitting, it can cause considerable discomfort, and in some cases – such as under-wired bras – may even be dangerous. A wide range of sports bras, knickers and underpants are available from retailers which are more suitable for riding than fashion garments may be. Bearing in mind the potential for embarrassment to some clients, teachers should broach this topic with discretion and tact.

Gloves

Gloves are not essential, but they do enable the pupil to keep a better grip on the reins and can help to prevent the occurrence of blisters on the fingers. Light-coloured gloves can also be a useful teaching aid, making it easier for the instructor to observe the position of the pupil's hands.

Body and back protectors

Wearing a body or back protector during jumping instruction is an optional choice for pupils, but it is strongly recommended that they do so.

JEWELLERY Jewellery should not be worn: earrings, bracelets, necklaces and rings should be removed before riding as these could cause serious injuries in the event of a fall. Pupils should be advised to leave such items at home, but as this advice is not always heeded, provision should be made for the safekeeping of such valuables during the lesson.

From top: correctly fitting a hat; adjusting and securing the retaining harness; too small a hat, and an overlarge hat. All protective headgear, whether the rider's or hired, should meet current safety standards

Whips

✔ Be firm where necessary, but try to avoid becoming bossy or behaving like a regimental sergeant major.

✔ A good teacher imparts reasons and facts: a poor instructor imparts neither.

It may sometimes be necessary for a pupil to carry a whip, but before being allowed to do so, it is essential that the teacher first spends some time explaining when and how it should be carried and used, in order to prevent its misuse or abuse.

Careful supervision may be needed particularly when teaching children, who may not appreciate the frightening effect a whip can have on a horse or pony if it is incorrectly handled; in addition, they may tend to use it as a substitute for leg aids, rather than as a means to reinforce the leg aid, used only as occasion requires it. When mounting and dismounting, the pupil should be taught to hold the whip with the reins in the left hand to avoid frightening the horse.

Types of whip

Short whips only should be used for jumping activities, and these are also more appropriate for children and less experienced riders. Long dressage whips should only be used by more advanced riders during flatwork instruction.

If the end of the whip has been damaged, resulting in the fibreglass core being exposed, it should not be used as it may cut the horse.

(Top row, from left) The correct way of carrying a short whip, incorrect way, and using a short whip
(Bottom row, from left in sequence) The correct way of transferring a short whip from left to right hand

Ability to carry a whip

The pupil should not be allowed or encouraged to carry a whip until his posture and co-ordination are sufficiently established to enable him to use the whip correctly when required, and to hold it quietly the rest of the time in such a manner that it is not upsetting or irritating to the horse.

Some horses are whip-shy, and in such cases a pupil should not carry one.

Carrying a whip

The teacher should explain and demonstrate the proper way of carrying a whip. He should also show the pupil how to change it over from left to right hand and vice versa quickly and easily, in such a way that the horse is not accidentally touched, or frightened by the action, and without risk of the rider becoming unbalanced or injuring himself.

Use of the whip

The pupil should be taught the correct use of the whip, touching, stroking, or tapping with it either just behind his leg, or on the horse's shoulder. The teacher should also explain under what circumstances it should be used, how hard, and in what situations it is appropriate to use it on either area of the horse's body. The pupil should be warned of the inadvisability and dangers of using a whip on the horse's quarters, flanks, head or neck.

If the teacher carries a whip of some description, whether short, long or a lunge whip, it should never be used to make a cracking noise or to hit the horse, as this may cause it to take fright. He should also be very aware of the alarming effect which any gestures he might make with it may have on the horse, and the consequences this may give rise to, and he should therefore take great care as to how he handles it.

(Top row, from left) The correct way of holding a long whip, and incorrect way
(Bottom row, from left in sequence) The correct way of transferring a long whip from left to right hand

Lungeing Equipment

✔ Side reins should always be used when lungeing a rider.

✔ Pupils' errors should not go uncorrected.

LUNGE WHIP The lunge whip should balance comfortably in the hand and not be so heavy that it becomes tiring to hold.

It is vital for both control and safety that suitable equipment, properly fitted and in good repair, is used for lessons on the lunge. In addition to a saddle and snaffle bridle, see opposite for the horse's equipment:

The teacher's dress

Whilst conducting a lunge lesson the teacher should dress in normal, smart attire, and always wear a hard hat. Gloves should also be worn, to provide a good grip on the lunge rein and to prevent friction burns and blisters. Spurs, if worn, should be removed.

Lungeing area

The lungeing area must be enclosed, and the surface should be level with good footing. Care should be taken to avoid lungeing too close to walls or fencing, as this will disturb the horse's gait and balance.

Safety

Lunge lessons should not be conducted in the school at the same time as other lessons unless the area is large enough to be safely divided. Correct and knowledgeable management of all lungeing equipment by the teacher is essential: in particular he should take care to:

- refrain from wrapping the lunge rein around his hand;
- ensure that the lunge rein does not become slack or drag along the ground, whether the horse is in movement or stationary;
- avoid sudden, abrupt movements with the whip;
- ensure that the side reins do not restrict forward movement, or are used to enforce a headcarriage.

LUNGE REIN The lunge rein should be a minimum length of 36-39ft (8–9m), and be attached to the central, swivelling ring of the lunge cavesson's noseband, as it controls forward movement, not the bend of the horse's neck. Spring clips are easier to attach and remove quickly than buckle fastenings; both should be mounted on a swivel to help prevent the lunge rein from becoming twisted. Cotton web or tubular linen lunge reins give a better grip than nylon web which tends to be slippery, and is also more likely to flap in a breeze.

Stirrup leathers should be secured to avoid the irons sliding down and banging against the horse's sides whilst it is being lunged without a rider

SIDE REINS Correctly fitted and adjusted side reins enhance the safety of all concerned by stabilising the balance of the horse, making control much easier, without inhibiting correct, free forward movement. They should be attached to the girth straps of the saddle at an equal height and not be allowed to slip downwards, and adjusted to be of equal length. When not in use they should either be removed entirely, or clipped to the front D-rings of the saddle (as shown here). Matching them in length is easier with hole and buckle adjustments than with sliding buckles.

LUNGE CAVESSON This should not be heavy, must fit snugly, and have a well-padded noseband to prevent chafing. The metal parts should be stainless steel for safety. The nose-piece should preferably be hinged in three places to ensure a closer, more comfortable fit and also allow for use on a number of horses.

The lunge cavesson should be fitted so that it does not interfere with the bit or restrict the horse's breathing, and both the noseband and jowl strap should be tightened sufficiently firmly that the cheekpiece(s) do not move, or ride up into the horse's eye. Remove the bridle noseband to ensure correct and comfortable fitting of the lunge cavesson.

BOOTS Due to the physical demands of working on a 20m-diameter circle for a sustained period of time, it is a wise precaution to fit brushing boots on all four of the horse's legs, even if it has excellent conformation and is not normally inclined to brush.

NECKSTRAP A breastplate or neckstrap is invaluable for the pupil to hold if he feels insecure, tired or unbalanced, and it can save the horse's mouth from much damage. If a neckstrap is used rather than a breastplate, a spur strap or similar should be looped through it, and then through one of the front D-rings on the saddle, to ensure that it does not slip forwards.

PART FOUR: Teaching

Considerations

Teaching Children

✔ Try to put your heart, interest and enthusiasm into each lesson.
✔ Be inventive to keep children and horses interested and stimulated.

Teaching children can be as satisfying and rewarding as teaching adult pupils, but in certain respects can be more demanding, stretching the teacher's skills and ingenuity to the full.

Age considerations

'Children' can generally be defined as pupils up to the age of sixteen. It is suggested that the minimum age at which pupils are accepted is five years, but it must be emphasised that at this age instruction will usually be very basic, aimed primarily at creating and maintaining confidence.

From the age of around seven years the child becomes both physically and mentally better able to cope with riding lessons, and instructional input can gradually become more complex and demanding.

Duration of lessons

Lessons for younger age groups should not be excessively long, as children will tire more quickly than adults. It is advisable to include individual exercises and work on school movements in walk during group lessons, because this helps to ensure that the strength and stamina of pupils are not overtaxed, as may happen if the ride is kept in trot for long periods.

Young children also have a short attention span: the instructor should be aware of this, plan lessons accordingly, and be prepared to adapt or alter the planned content if signs of fatigue or loss of concentration are noticed. It should be borne in mind that children may already be a little tired if the riding lesson is conducted after school.

The following are proposed guidelines as to how long a lesson might be expected to last – although at the instructor's discretion, some pupils may be able to manage longer periods than that suggested for their particular age group:

- 5–7 years: up to 30 minutes;
- 7–16 years: up to 1 hour.

Competitiveness

For the majority of children, riding is an enjoyable leisure activity, so whilst the teacher should encourage a desire in his pupils to increase their knowledge and improve their skills, the 'fun' aspect should not be neglected: indeed it should be emphasised.

Most children are inclined to be competitive, and this tendency can be a useful teaching tool for the teacher. For instance, it can help to inject an element of fun into a lesson: incorporating little games or a quiz into the lesson is often a good idea, perhaps testing the children on what

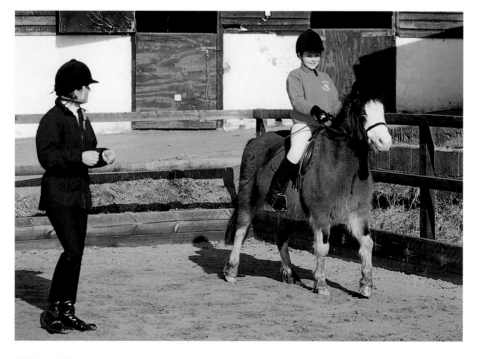

Teacher showing sensible control in a child's lesson with the accent on safety

different bits of tack are called, or on the points of the pony. While children and ponies are resting physically, their interest and competitive spirit can still be engaged.

It is essential however, that competitiveness is not allowed to get out of hand: any simple games or competitions which are incorporated into a lesson need to be carefully organised with regard to the safety of the riders and the welfare of the ponies. In group lessons, equal encouragement should be given to 'losers' as well as to 'winners', and games selected which offer weaker members of the lesson a chance of success, otherwise such pupils may become disheartened and negative in their attitude.

CONSIDERATION   During lessons, the teacher should try to develop the child's respect and consideration for the pony he is riding, and discourage abusive actions such as pulling sharply on the reins, excessive kicking or use of the whip. These often occur as a direct result of frustration at an inability to do something, so rather than just reprimanding such behaviour, the teacher should first explain why it is unacceptable, and then offer constructive assistance to help resolve the difficulty which led to the incident.

Remember that above all, safety is paramount, and the teacher will need to be particularly vigilant with children, whose concentration span may not match that of adults.

Teaching technique

For safety and to give confidence, younger children will benefit from being led by a helper. Explanations and instructions should be kept as uncomplicated as possible when teaching pupils of any age, but this is especially important where younger children are concerned, whose vocabulary and depth of understanding will be much more limited than that of adults. They will also find it difficult to cope if asked to make several corrections simultaneously, so the teacher must also be prepared to concentrate on one priority at a time.

Before beginning any exercise, the teacher should first briefly describe it, and assure himself that each of the pupils understands what is required. He should also explain in simple terms any specific difficulties which may arise during the exercise, and how to deal with them. Even from a fairly early age, children can be encouraged to think problems through for themselves, by asking them to comment on what they felt went right or wrong during each exercise, and how they could improve on it the next time. This also has the effect of making the lesson more interactive and enjoyable for the child, whilst at a deeper

Where games and competitions are incorporated into lessons, these must always be appropriate to the pupil's level of ability, and take into account the pony's temperament

level, what they have learnt is likely to have been more thoroughly absorbed.

The teacher must always to be positive, and should always be generous with praise and encouragement, particularly when a pupil is trying hard, even if his efforts do not always meet with success. Constant criticism is negative in its effect, as is sarcasm or making fun of a child, which will foster resentment and hostility, and may possibly result in him being tempted to take out his feelings on the pony. Favouritism should also be avoided, or concentrating excessively on the more adept pupils in group lessons: the teacher should try to spread his attention as equally as possible amongst all the pupils.

Teaching Children

MOUNTED EXERCISES

Exercises such as Toe Touching (**1**), Dismounting (**2–3**) and Round the World (**4–11**) help develop balance and confidence. Most children enjoy performing these, although they should only be attempted on ponies of a steady disposition unlikely to be upset by the pupil's movements. The pony should be held by the teacher or a competent assistant in order to maintain control, and they should be close enough to provide a supporting hand to the pupil if necessary.

The toe touching exercise can be varied by asking the pupil to touch other parts of his, or the pony's body or saddlery; by turning it into a 'Simon Says' exercise it becomes a fun way of learning the names of the parts of the pony and equipment.

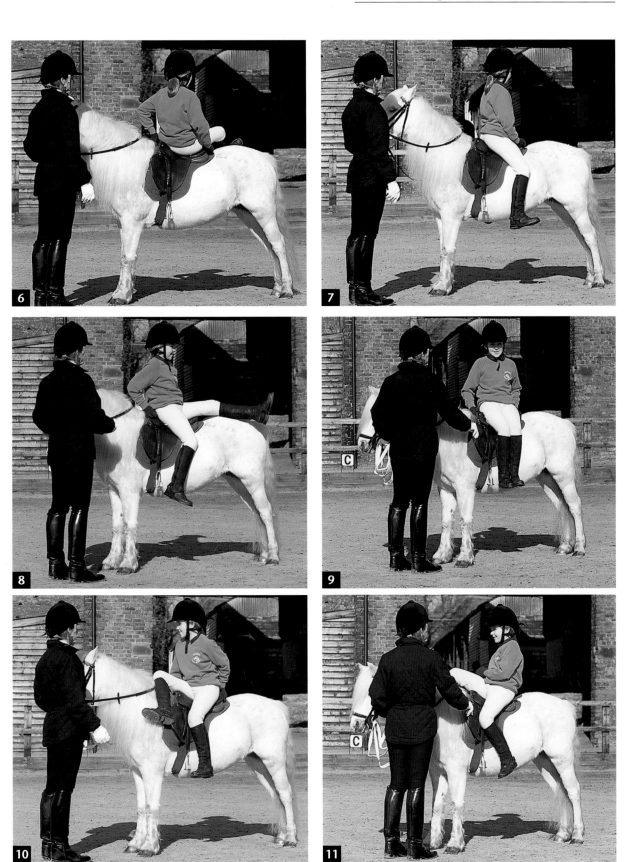

Teaching Adults

✔ If a pupil expresses reservations about your theories on equitation, do not treat this as a challenge to your authority or knowledge, rather, congratulate yourself on having succeeded in arousing the pupil's interest and awakening his analytical abilities.

✔ Be ready to support a pupil on dismounting: he may be more fatigued than he realises, and his knees may buckle as his feet touch the ground.

For lessons to be enjoyable as well as constructive, the teacher should take into consideration the following points when teaching adult pupils:

■ Adults may be more nervous and self-conscious than children: they may be more easily embarrassed, and are often worried that they might look foolish in front of others, or are afraid of failure. The teacher should never use these inclinations as a lever to persuade the pupil to attempt an exercise which he is not confident about; indeed, he should always try to preserve the pupil's dignity, selecting exercises that are suitable for his age and ability.

■ Naturally, adults will be able to absorb more technical and complicated explanations (providing they are made clear) than children, and are often interested in discussing and analysing aspects of equitation; this can make teaching them a fascinating and absorbing challenge for the knowledgeable instructor. However, he should take care to ensure that the depth and complexity of his explanations are appropriate to the level and experience of the pupil; he must also remember that learning or developing equestrian skills is concerned as much with practice as theory. He should therefore try to fit the maximum amount of practical work/riding into each lesson, keeping theory to a working minimum and avoiding unnecessarily lengthy or involved discussions.

■ Tact and diplomacy should be exercised with adult pupils, who may become resentful of a bullying, hectoring manner, or if they perceive that they are being humoured or patronised – particularly if they are more senior in years to the teacher. The teacher should respect his pupil, treating him as an equal and never insult his intelligence.

■ Adults may often experience difficulties in mastering a correct position in the saddle, due to lack of suppleness and the acquisition of poor postural habits over the years. It may be helpful for the teacher to suggest a few dismounted suppling exercises which may be performed between lessons to help remedy this.

■ Pupils unaccustomed to riding, or unable to ride daily, may find it physically demanding. The teacher should therefore allow a sufficient working-in period at the beginning of the lesson as well as frequent rest periods, and should avoid asking pupils to make excessively strenuous efforts which can lead to pain, distress or even injury.

■ The teacher should be considerate of the needs of more mature adults who may suffer from age-related physical problems such as arthritis, less efficient blood circulation, some impairment of hearing, and slower reaction times. A mounting block is strongly recommended, to assist the more mature rider in mounting, as well as to reduce any likelihood of the pupil landing heavily on the horse's back.

■ Adults are often more cautious than children, and may be nervous or apprehensive because they are more aware of the risk of injury and its consequences on their personal lives. A sensible rate of progress, clear explanations of all procedures, attention to correct, secure posture and adhering to safe teaching practices will do much to alleviate any fears the pupil may have.

■ The teacher should discuss the pupil's riding experience and ambitions, so that lessons can be structured accordingly. Setting short-term, more easily attainable goals to act as a progressive series of stepping stones will prevent the pupil from becoming discouraged, instead promoting in him a sense of achievement as he masters each step.

ADULT RIDERS Particular care should be taken in the selection of a suitable horse for more mature riders, who may be experiencing the onset of various physical infirmities; it should also be borne in mind that the consequences of a fall may be far more serious than for someone younger. Consequently it is essential that a mount should be chosen which is not excessively wide in its barrel, which is steady and reliable in its temperament, obedient to the aids and gives a smooth and comfortable ride.

The teacher should also be aware of the difficulties, and indeed discomfort, which some exercises may impose for a pupil with a reduced range of movement, and be both realistic and sensible in his requests. Feedback from the pupil should be encouraged as to what he feels able to manage comfortably, and such comments should always be heeded, and the work adapted accordingly.

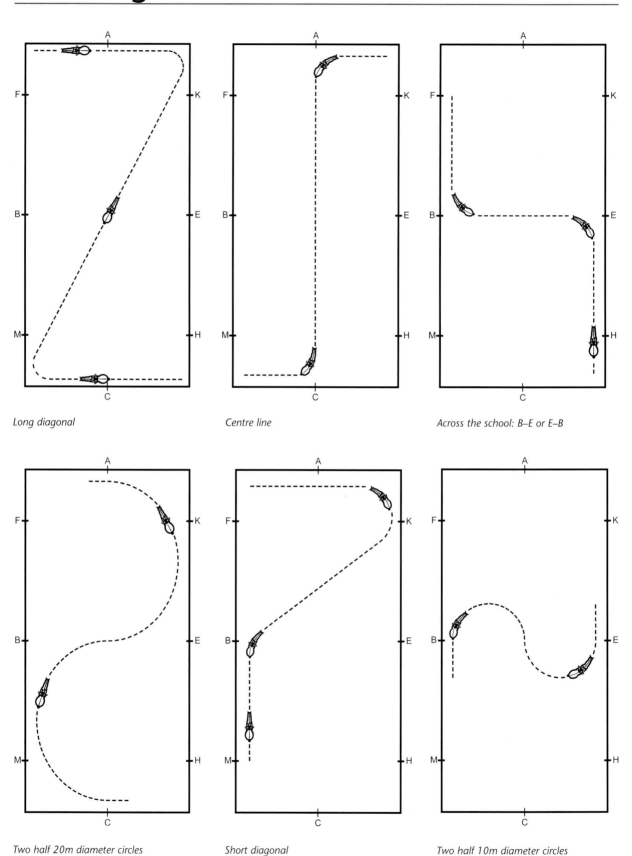

Long diagonal

Centre line

Across the school: B–E or E–B

Two half 20m diameter circles

Short diagonal

Two half 10m diameter circles

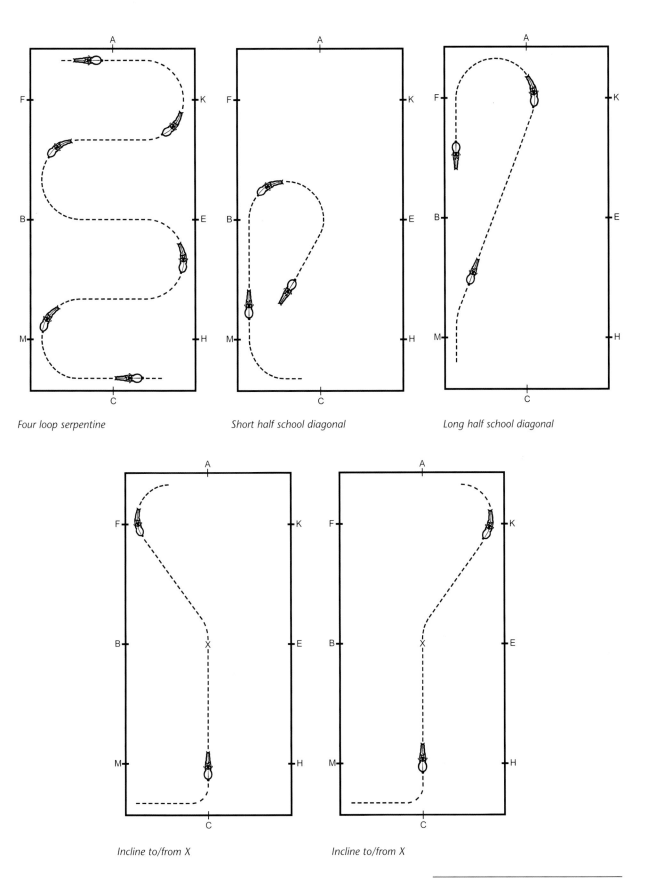

Four loop serpentine

Short half school diagonal

Long half school diagonal

Incline to/from X

Incline to/from X

Nervous Riders

✔ Never try to manufacture a fall.

✔ Fear slows and inhibits the learning process. It can literally be physically paralysing, to the exclusion of all rational thought or action.

✔ Place emphasis on what can be – and is – achieved, not on what cannot be, or hasn't been achieved during a lesson.

Teaching nervous pupils requires great sensitivity, patience, tact and skill on the part of the teacher. He should discuss with his pupil all those causes which may be contributing to his anxieties in order to determine how best he may help him overcome them. Fears which may seem ridiculous, irrational or trivial to the teacher may be very real to the pupil, so should not be ridiculed, but treated seriously and with understanding.

Common causes of nervousness

Insecurity: For the pupil who is new to riding, the movement of the horse – even in walk – may feel alarming, disturbing his balance; he may also feel nervous as to his ability to control his mount.

Previous riding history: A pupil who has previously had a frightening experience, even if this has not resulted in an injury, will understandably be apprehensive of a similar

The choice of a steady, quiet horse is vital for nervous pupils if their confidence is to develop

occurrence happening again. Unsympathetic teaching, with insufficient regard for sensible and safe teaching practices, is often responsible for causing nervousness in pupils.

Unfamiliarity: Pupils unused to horses may find their sheer size and strength daunting, especially when this is coupled with a lack of understanding of how the equine mind works.

Fear of injury: Even a pupil who has never been injured as a result of a riding accident, may fear this possibility.

Temperament: Some people are naturally less physically bold in their temperament than others: those who are inclined to be highly strung or have a very active imagination may also be more nervous than pupils without these characteristics.

Teaching nervous pupils

- The horse allocated to the pupil must be suitable: not over-large or strong, a known quantity with a steady, placid temperament, and a comfortable way of moving which will not be unseating for the rider.

- Arrange for the pupil to ride the same horse for several lessons: familiarity may help to develop confidence.

- If the pupil is currently on a class lesson, suggest a few private lessons when he will be able to progress at his own speed without feeling any pressure to keep up with others in the group; this will also mean that any specific problems or fears can be addressed more successfully. Moving the pupil to a less advanced group may also be a solution, but can make him feel that he is being 'demoted', giving rise to feelings of failure and uselessness.

- During private tuition, remain as close to the horse as possible, since the pupil will derive comfort from the knowledge that should he experience difficulties, the teacher can step in and take control of the situation.

- Overcoming fear or nervousness relies on the pupil being able to trust totally the teacher's judgement as to his ability to perform safely any exercise or movement: such faith must never be abused. The teacher should emphasise to the pupil that he will not be asked to do anything which might endanger him.

Some pupils may gain security, stability and confidence from holding the front arch of the saddle with one hand, particularly whilst working in more active gaits such as sitting trot. The lightest of grips on the saddle is preferable to the rider using the reins for support and balance

NERVES   Nerves can play a role in the success or otherwise of pupils taking part in examinations or competitions. Whilst some may find it a stimulating challenge which can provide an extra edge, others may find it a nervewracking experience which consequently detracts from their performance.

The teacher should strive to ensure that the pupil is prepared to a level a little above that at which he is competing or being examined at, and has been fully briefed as to correct procedure on the day. No matter how trivial or groundless the pupil's anxieties may seem, the teacher should not mock them, but rather should try to allay excessive worries by discussing those areas which his pupil feels apprehensive about.

For many pupils the greatest fear is that they may make a fool of themselves in front of complete strangers; in such cases, it may be helpful to encourage them to participate in group lessons especially if they are well attended by onlookers. If possible, it can also be beneficial to have a mock rehearsal as part of the pupil's final preparation in order to boost confidence and help eliminate lingering doubts.

- Encourage the pupil to think positively about what he wishes the horse to do, and how to make this happen.

- Progress with nervous pupils must not be rushed: each stage must be thoroughly mastered before moving on to the next.

- The teacher should explain, and if necessary demonstrate, each new movement, describing the reasons for doing it, how to achieve it, and the sensations which will be felt, before asking the pupil to attempt it.

- A correct posture in the saddle will enable the rider to be secure and effective in his control of the horse, so great attention must be paid to this aspect. Demonstration of the benefits of correct posture may also help to reassure the pupil.

- If the pupil has a specific fear – for example, that the horse might buck or bolt – the teacher should seek to reassure him that this is extremely unlikely to happen. Further confidence may be instilled by working the pupil in a smaller area with the teacher nearby.

- Dismounted lectures on aspects of horse management, both theoretical and practical in nature, may help. Learning how the equine brain thinks, and how to handle horses safely, can do a great deal to overcome nervousness which may be due in large part simply to lack of knowledge and familiarity with them.

- At the end of the lesson, the teacher should briefly recap all the positive things the pupil has accomplished. However minor these might have been, they may represent a major achievement for the pupil, who will then approach the next lesson with a more positive attitude.

Nervous Riders

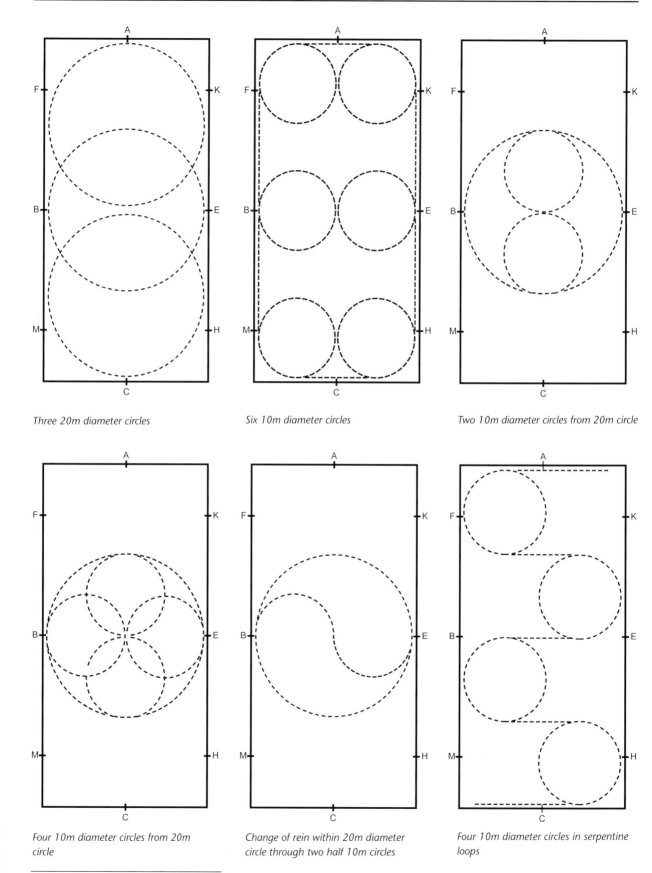

Three 20m diameter circles

Six 10m diameter circles

Two 10m diameter circles from 20m circle

Four 10m diameter circles from 20m circle

Change of rein within 20m diameter circle through two half 10m circles

Four 10m diameter circles in serpentine loops

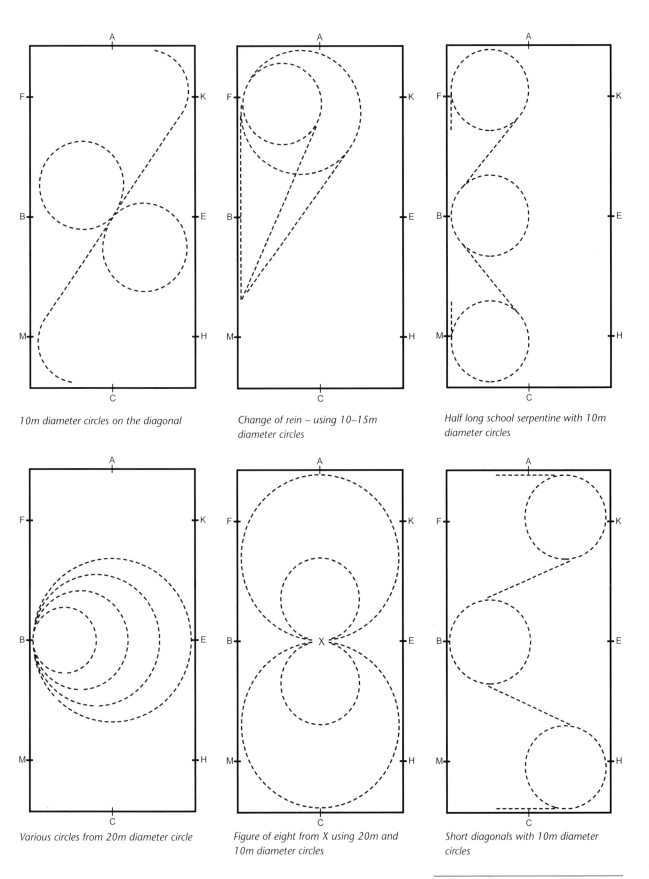

10m diameter circles on the diagonal

Change of rein – using 10–15m diameter circles

Half long school serpentine with 10m diameter circles

Various circles from 20m diameter circle

Figure of eight from X using 20m and 10m diameter circles

Short diagonals with 10m diameter circles

Disabled and Handicapped Riders

✔ It's not what the rider can't achieve but what he can that's important.
✔ The smallest success can be a major achievement.

Riding can have tremendous benefits for riders with special needs: a mentally and physically stimulating challenge, it can bring the rewards of improved co-ordination and balance, a feeling of freedom and independence, and increased self-confidence. New capabilities begin to take precedence over long-accepted disabilities, and new relationships may be forged with both people and horses.

The following are offered only as brief guidelines regarding the tuition of disabled pupils. Disabled riders have their own organisation, run by a wonderful band of hard-working volunteers, and those interested in finding out more about this aspect of teaching should contact the Riding for the Disabled Association (see page 126), and must use their current manuals.

The horse/pony

Careful thought needs to be given to the horses or ponies which are used. Ideally a sensible trial should be given to them before acceptance. Suitable horses should be:

- sound;
- sensible, steady, unflappable and kind in temperament;
- forward-going, as some riders may lack, or be limited in, the use of their legs – although horses should never be 'gassy' or excitable;
- regular and rhythmic in their gaits, and without stiffness in their action;
- comfortable in their action, and able to move smoothly through transitions, as the rider's balance may be precarious;
- obedient and responsive to verbal commands as well as to physical aids.

A selection of heights and widths will need to be available to accommodate a variety of riders with differing problems: narrower horses/ponies will be required for some, whilst others will fare better on animals which are broader across the back, giving a better base of support. Horses in excess of 15.2hh will make it difficult for helpers to assist mounted riders, and their size may frighten those who are nervous.

Horses/ponies used frequently by disabled pupils can become bored with their work, so they should also be regularly schooled and taken for hacks by able-bodied riders. This helps to keep their work varied and interesting, and to ensure that they remain supple and obedient.

Disabled and Handicapped Riders

Equipment

Each horse's saddlery should be adapted as recommended for the needs of the individual rider; a breastplate with a leather handle stitched onto it can often be a helpful addition. Otherwise normal saddlery, as employed by able-bodied riders, is generally used as far as possible. On occasions this may not be either suitable or safe and alternatives may be needed (see current RDA manuals); for example:

- Western saddles: these may be appropriate for some riders as they are wider across the seat than English-style saddles and have a high pommel in front, and so can be useful for pupils with spina bifida or riders paralysed from the waist down.
- Australian stock saddles: these can also be appropriate in some circumstances, having two high knee pads which can prevent the legs of riders with tight inner thigh muscles from creeping upwards.
- Where saddles may be too wide, an anti-cast roller may be used, with the rider sitting behind it and using the arch as a handle to hold on to.
- Side saddles may also be helpful for one-limbed riders, or for those who are tight in the inner thigh muscles – allowing them to sit with their legs much closer together.
- Ladder reins, with rungs across them.
- Coloured reins for riders who cannot remember left from right.

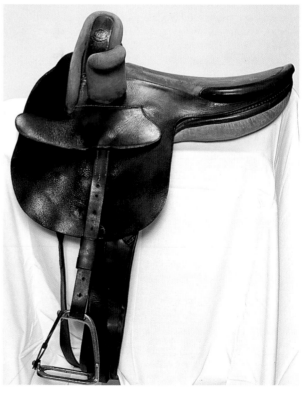

The opportunity to ride can give those with special needs a sense of freedom, mobility and independence as well as being physically beneficial. (top left) A simple device, like the reins with loops attached shown here, can allow a rider to shorten and lengthen the reins with relative ease

Far left: A specialist saddle with a handle, and bucket stirrups to help prevent a rider's feet slipping through the irons.

Left: Side saddles may be helpful for some riders; this one is fitted with a safety iron

Above: A suitable horse, equipped with a neck strap and a saddle with safety irons. The mounting block is sturdy and non-slip

- Seat savers for those riders who may suffer from pressure sores when riding.
- Bucket stirrups, to prevent a rider's feet from slipping through the stirrup irons.

Additional facilities include:

- Mounting blocks or platforms with ramps for wheelchair access. The use of mounting blocks and platforms is to be encouraged for the ease and safety of pupils in both mounting and dismounting, and to reduce any danger of strain on the horse's back, or damage to the saddle. Mounting blocks should be designed so that pupils can mount from either side of the horse. They must be large enough for two people to stand on at once, be stable, non-slip and have no sharp edges or corners. Platforms should be a minimum of 1.2m (4ft) square with a non-slip ramp with a gentle gradient and a handrail up to, and around, the top. The 'open' edge should be clearly defined.
- Mounting pits: these have the advantage that a rider approaches on one level. The pit should be well-drained, and not so deep that helpers need to stoop to assist a rider. The gradient in and out should be gentle.
- A safe, enclosed area, in which riders can establish confidence.

Safety

✔ Better a boring lesson than an unsafe one.

✔ The ages and the physical ability of clients must be considered when any physical exercises are requested.

✔ It is the teacher's responsibility to assure himself that any person delegated to assist him is capable of carrying out the assigned task in a safe, competent and knowledgeable manner. He should ensure that this assistant is aged sixteen years or over.

The safety of pupils is of paramount importance, and it is the teacher's responsibility to establish the following parameters:

- To ensure that pupils are dressed correctly (see Clothing).
- To ensure that they are safely and suitably mounted.
- He should not ask – or give permission to – any pupil to perform any act of horse management or riding which, to the best of his knowledge, is not within the capacity of that pupil.
- To point out any known risks or hazards, and stress the importance of adhering to correct safety procedures at all times.
- To ensure that safe teaching methods are used.
- To be constantly vigilant for signs of tiredness in riders, and fatigue or fractiousness in horses.
- To maintain good ride organisation and discipline.

Ride organisation

When pupils are working as a ride, the teacher should place horses in a sensible order, with those which are more free-moving or have a longer stride positioned at the front, to avoid any unsafe bunching up of the rest of the group. The most proficient rider should be placed at the head of the ride as leading file: with groups of less experienced pupils it may be advantageous for a capable member of staff to take this role. The leading file – whether a member of staff or a pupil – should be briefed to adopt a speed which as far as possible will not cause unreasonable difficulties for the rest of the ride in maintaining correct distances.

Before asking pupils to move off from halt to take up their positions in the ride, the teacher should first explain how they can judge if they are a correct and safe distance from the horse in front: either a half, a whole, or two horses' lengths apart according to his instructions. Since not all horses will be perfectly matched in length of stride/gait speed, the teacher should also explain how each pupil can maintain this distance by:

- riding more deeply into corners to avoid getting too close to the horse in front;
- cutting across a corner in order to close up distances;
- increasing/reducing the gait speed, or returning to a slower gait if necessary;
- circling away from the ride if working in open order.

When asking the ride to execute any school figure, movement or transition the teacher should ensure that:

- his voice can be clearly heard by all the pupils;

Safe distances must be maintained between horses at all times

(Left) If the ride is halted so as to permit each rider in turn to attempt a particular exercise or movement, encourage those waiting their turn to watch. This can be as valuable a learning process for the pupil as actually performing it himself

(Below) Good posture is safe, secure, effective and the foundation of all ridden work

■ that the pupils are given sufficient advance warning (preliminary command) of the exercise, and adequate time in which to prepare before the command to commence (executive command) is given.

Other points for consideration

■ All new pupils should be assessed in order to determine the most appropriate group for them to join.

■ Before asking pupils to ride various exercises and school figures, first be sure that they understand what is required by giving a clear explanation, followed if necessary by a demonstration either on foot or on horseback. Pupils should then ride the movement satisfactorily in walk before attempting it in faster gaits.

■ A correct posture in the saddle is also a safe and effective one, and provides the pupil with a sound foundation upon which to build.

■ Basic ability and a safe posture must be established at slower gaits before encouraging pupils to attempt more demanding work.

■ Remember that if pupils are allowed to become bored and inattentive, accidents are more likely to occur.

■ Pupils must never be left unattended/unsupervised or outside the range/vision of the teacher during the course of a lesson, or of a competent assistant when taking horses to or from the school.

■ Assistants should be on hand to assist pupils in bringing horses to the school, and with helping them to check and adjust the saddlery, and mount. The teacher should, however, take the precaution of checking for himself that all saddlery is safe and correctly adjusted before permitting any rider to move off. A second check should be made ten minutes into the lesson, to ensure that girths are still sufficiently tight. Assistants should also be available to help pupils in returning horses to their stables at the end of a lesson.

OBSERVATION If any of the horses in the group are unknown to the teacher, he should find out in advance if these are known to exhibit any tendencies or mannerisms such as nipping, biting or kicking, which could pose a risk to pupils. Similarly, when teaching any pupil he does not know, he should try to ascertain, through questioning, that pupil's previous riding experience, and any physical problems, difficulties or anxieties he may have.

It is important for the teacher to possess the ability to 'read' the body language of both horses and riders, being quick to note signs of temper, irritation or nervousness, and to react appropriately in order to avert the possibility of an accident occurring as a result.

PART FIVE

Teaching Skills

Lesson Structure

✔ Explain to pupils the importance of maintaining safe distances between horses – don't merely request it.

✔ The use of school figures and movements should be a means to an end, not an end in itself.

Whether teaching individual or group lessons, the teacher needs to be inventive and ingenious in keeping both pupil and horse mentally and physically occupied.

Content and structure

Although the teacher may have a particular theme he wishes to work on during a lesson, he should be fairly flexible as to content. His observation of pupils and horses during the initial warming-up period should have given him a fairly clear idea of their strengths and weaknesses, and the priorities to which he needs to give his attention. He should therefore avoid committing himself to any particular theme in advance of taking the lesson, although he may find it helpful to adopt the following broad lesson plan:

1 The teacher introduces himself to the ride.
2 Pupil(s) mount: safety checks of tack.
3 Warming up: assessment of pupil(s) and horse(s) and check tack.
4 The teacher explains the points he wants to work on during the lesson.
5 Work on specific exercises/figures/movements to achieve these goals. Each one may be broken down into simple steps: explanation; demonstration; check pupil's understanding of what is required; practice; discuss; repeat.
6 Conclusion of lesson: discussion of what has been taught: pupil's questions and answers.

Below and right: Figure, drill and formation riding can help pupils to develop their ability to ride independently and effectively

Figure, drill and formation riding

Figure riding is an excellent way of teaching the pupil the correct and effective use of the natural aids; it will also keep both him and his horse mentally and physically alert, and it prevents the teacher from becoming (or appearing to be) bored. He should encourage accuracy in the execution of all figures and movements, using the fixed letter markers around the school, and where appropriate, movable accessories such as poles, cones or Bloks to help riders achieve this.

Drills and formation riding when teaching groups can also be useful in helping to make lessons interesting, stimulating and enjoyable. With larger groups, it helps to prevent riders from becoming bored, waiting whilst others perform individual movements in succession and develops their ability to ride independently and effectively. It has the added

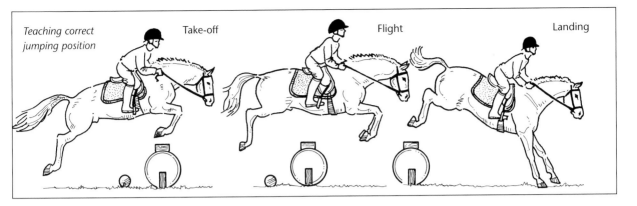

Teaching correct jumping position   Take-off   Flight   Landing

benefit of discouraging horses from developing a 'nose-to-tail' mentality causing them to become nappy.

All exercises/movements/figures should be explained, and if necessary demonstrated, before asking the pupil to execute them, and they should not be beyond the ability of either rider or horse to perform. The teacher should begin with simpler movements, even with more advanced pupils, gradually increasing the degree of difficulty in a logical progression. Some exercises/movements/figures may initially appear pointless to the pupil, so the teacher should be at pains to explain why each exercise is selected, and what benefits are to be gained by horse and rider.

CONSIDERATIONS

- A knowledgeable teacher will select those exercises, school figures and movements which will be of most benefit in furthering his pupil's understanding and ability: he will not employ them at random merely for the sake of something to do.
- The teacher should take care not to focus all his attention on one rider and neglect others when taking group lessons.
- When pupils are performing individual exercises on the flat and when jumping, the teacher should ensure that he maintains control and observes the whole ride.
- Introducing an entirely new subject late in the lesson is never a good idea: pupil and horse may both be tired, and there may not be enough time in which to teach it successfully.
- Finish a lesson early if the pupil has achieved all the objectives set for him during that session. If it is necessary to 'fill in' a small amount of allotted time, employ it usefully in discussion of what has been taught and learnt.
- Teachers should try to keep lessons running to time as far as possible: if a lesson overruns, all those following will begin late. This can be irritating for clients, can wreak havoc with yard routine, and means that horses end up working longer hours than they should.
- Enough time should be left at the end of the lesson to answer any questions pupils may have.

Pupils can initially be taught the correct jumping position whilst at halt before practising it with the horse in movement

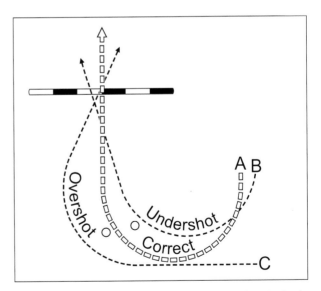

Teaching correct approaches to a fence can also be done in simple stages – over a single pole on the ground initially. The teacher should explain why 'A' is correct and the problems which may arise from taking approach 'B' or 'C', explaining how to avoid these by planning turns and looking towards the pole to ensure accuracy. If the pupil has already been taught how to ride school figures accurately there should be little difficulty in mastering this. Markers may be used to encourage an accurate turn and straight approach

Teaching Aids

✔ Try to finish your lessons on a good note when your pupil(s) have achieved some degree of success, and whilst they are still eager.

✔ Advise pupils not to fear mistakes. Mistakes are not failures; they are essential to the learning process.

✔ There is no substitute for experience.

The teacher has various teaching aids at his disposal which can be usefully employed to help illustrate or demonstrate points of equitation: nevertheless they can prove to be a double-edged sword if not exercised with caution.

Imagery

Imagery can be a powerful tool with which the teacher can help the pupil master new skills, overcome postural difficulties, understand more complex concepts, and develop his sense of 'feel'. The teacher does, however, need to be careful not to allow himself to become so carried away with his own rhetoric that he neglects to offer clear, constructive and practical instruction, or causes confusion as to his meaning. It must always be remembered that a phrase or description which is meaningful to one individual might be totally incomprehensible to another; furthermore, inexperienced pupils may be inclined to interpret his words in too literal a manner.

Demonstration

On occasion the teacher may find that riding the pupil's horse to demonstrate a movement or principle of equitation is of assistance in helping him to understand it, especially if the pupil lacks the imagination or experience to visualise a verbal explanation. However, the teacher should be wary of spending more time on the horse than is necessary for the purposes of demonstration.

Videos

Video equipment and facilities, where available, can be an invaluable aid to both teacher and pupil in analysing problems and corrections. It is important, however, that the pupil is not allowed to become over-obsessed with trivia.

Music

Music can be a wonderful teaching aid for all levels of riders, if it is carefully selected and not allowed to drown out the teacher's voice (see Riding to Music, page 106).

Left: Riding the pupil's horse to demonstrate a movement or principle of equitation can be a useful way of helping a pupil to understand the points the teacher is trying to make and of clearing up any confusions

Top right: The use of differing and brightly coloured bandages can make it easier for pupils when observing a horse to distinguish the particular sequences of movement of its legs in each of the gaits

WALK

TROT

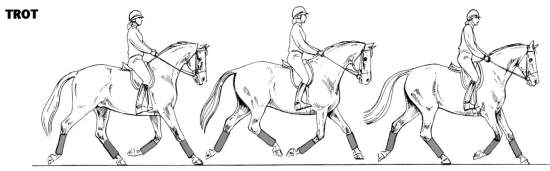

CANTER

Praise

The teacher must be quick to recognise and praise effort and improvement, however small, otherwise the pupil may quickly become disheartened, feeling that the teacher's objectives are beyond his scope to achieve. Praise, when it is perceived to have been earned, will encourage the pupil and increase his motivation – yet if it is given too freely, without regard as to whether improvement/effort has been shown, it soon becomes meaningless and will encourage the pupil to become complacent and sloppy.

Feedback

Careful questioning of the pupil, both during and at the end of a lesson, enables the teacher to determine how well his tuition has been absorbed and understood, and to ensure there have been no errors in communication.

The pupil may also have many questions for the teacher concerning what he has been taught. This two-way exchange helps the teacher to establish a rapport with his pupil, and it can also help to give him a new perspective on, or even clarify, any difficulties or anxieties the pupil has been experiencing. The teacher must therefore be prepared to listen to, and to answer all these queries, and he should reply to each as fully as he is able, in the simplest and clearest possible terms. He should try to avoid the use of jargon: his task is to enlighten the pupil, not further confuse him or attempt to impress him with his own superior knowledge.

These question and answer sessions have another important benefit, in that they afford both horses and pupils the opportunity to rest, either in halt, or walking on a long rein, depending on the weather and climatic conditions.

Maintaining Motivation

✔ Remember that the pursuit of the finer points of equitation may be of less importance to your pupils than it is to you: they may also have other hobbies and interests.

✔ A desire to learn and improve cannot be forced upon a pupil: it is something which first needs to be stimulated and then carefully nurtured.

One of the more difficult tasks which can present itself to the riding teacher is that of maintaining motivation in his pupils week after week.

Setting personal goals

Personal goals vary widely from one pupil to the next: it may be to master a particular movement, to achieve sufficient competence to go out for a hack, to be able to tackle small fences with confidence, take part in a competition, or ultimately to purchase a horse of his own.

The teacher must be sympathetic to each individual's goals, however humble they may be, and should offer support and encouragement as well as constructive tuition towards these ends. He should never belittle the pupil's aspirations, even if, realistically, he is unlikely to attain them: it is the constant striving towards a goal, however distant, which helps to provide the pupil with the motivation and incentive to persist.

However, to prevent the pupil from becoming disillusioned or disheartened, the teacher should also encourage him to work towards short-term, more easily attainable goals which can be viewed as a series of stepping stones towards achieving his ultimate ambition.

Although pupils should not feel they are under any compulsion to study towards and take examinations, they can be made aware of the existence of the ABRS Equitation and Stable Management Tests, and if they are interested in taking these, then they should be encouraged to do so. These tests provide an excellent yardstick by which pupils can measure their progress – and as success is achieved at each level, tangible proof of their efforts is provided in the form of a certificate. Each success is also an incentive to work towards the next level. (See also Appendix 1, page 124.)

The riding teacher

It is also important for the riding teacher to sustain his own motivation. He may quickly become jaded, particularly if he has a heavy teaching load, falling into a dull, formulaic style of teaching, making no real effort in lessons, and with little or no analysis of how he might help his pupils overcome any difficulties they encounter, or to progress further. His attitude will rapidly become apparent to his pupils, who may either lose interest themselves, or seek instruction elsewhere. More seriously, it can also lead to hasty and incorrect assumptions and the adoption of unsafe practices, which could physically endanger those he is teaching.

He should therefore make the effort, when his schedule permits, to watch others riding and teaching, and he should also go on courses and take advantage of training opportunities which may arise from time to time. Pupils will benefit from the revitalised enthusiasm, fresh ideas, insight and knowledge which he will be able to bring to his teaching as a result. Periodically swapping group lessons with other instructors may also help. Since a good instructor will keep his clients coming back each week eager to learn more, it is also in an employer's interests to encourage such practices.

SPECIAL EVENTS The organisation of special events is also helpful in maintaining enthusiasm, and can often add an extra dimension to, or insight into the pupil's riding activities. These might include:

- **Lectures and demonstrations** These might cover a variety of subjects of interest to pupils; they could be given either by a member of staff or by an invited guest 'expert'.
- **Courses** These may vary in length from two days to a week, and enable pupils to profit from the opportunity to ride on a daily basis. In addition to formal riding tuition, such courses might also include hacking, lectures, demonstrations, competitions and supervised stable management activities. 'Own a pony' days or weeks, organised along similar lines, also usually prove very popular with children, who are allocated a particular pony to ride and help care for throughout the duration of the course.
- **Client competitions** As with taking tests and examinations, the prospect of a competition ahead can help give tuition a greater direction and purpose. These are often popular with clients who, not owning a horse themselves, might otherwise never have the opportunity to compete.

Teaching Style

✔ Not everyone shares the same sense of humour, so exercise care in its use.
✔ The teacher should have the progress, safety and enjoyment of his pupil at heart, and not inflate his own ego or pander to his own sense of superiority.
✔ Do not be snappy or short-tempered with your pupils.

Teachers should try to develop their own individual teaching style rather than copying the idiosyncrasies of others: imitatation may be the sincerest form of flattery, but it is rarely a successful formula for teaching. At best it may appear ridiculous, false and contrived, at worst it may interfere with the teacher's ability to communicate clearly and honestly with the pupil.

Humour

Humour can be a useful way of breaking the ice, or of lightening the mood and relieving tension. The teacher must, however, laugh *with*, and not at the pupil: humour should never be at the rider's expense, nor should it degenerate into sarcasm, as this will only alienate pupils rather than earn their trust, and will invariably lead to the loss of their respect. Practical jokes can be dangerous, and are to be avoided.

Posture

Some consideration needs to be given as to the way in which the teacher projects his individual teaching style. He should try to sound enthusiastic: a dull monotone will fail to encourage or inspire the pupil, and any praise issued in such a fashion will sound half-hearted and lacking in sincerity. Like an actor, the teacher's posture is also important, and can be used effectively to illustrate, through gesture and attitude, many of the points he wishes to make. It will also reveal much of his own subconscious feelings – and not always favourable ones: for example, constantly looking down and dragging his feet not only affects voice projection and good observation, but will infer to the pupil that he either lacks confidence in himself, is bored with the lesson, or cares little about his pupils.

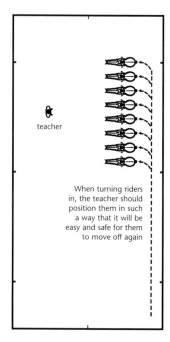

When turning riders in, the teacher should position them in such a way that it will be easy and safe for them to move off again

teacher

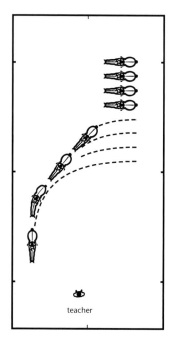

teacher

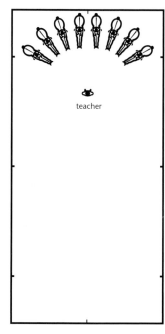

teacher

To ask the group to turn in and line up, the teacher should tell the leading file to turn inwards at a given marker and halt on the inside track/three-quarter line and the rest of the ride to turn inwards and form a line on the left/right of the person ahead

When the ride moves off again the teacher must ensure that he is not standing directly in the way

When addressing the ride in halt, the teacher will find it easiest to gain and keep their attention if they are positioned in such a way that they can see as well as hear him

Communication

✔ Never use twenty words when ten will do.

✔ Sometimes pupils will require more detailed or lengthy explanations. When this happens, be careful not to lose track of the point you are trying to make.

✔ How you say something can be as important as what you say.

One of the most important teaching tools at the teacher's command is his voice: effectively used, it can do more than merely communicate information. For safety, and if the pupil is to gain any benefit, it is vital that he can hear the teacher's voice. Sometimes conditions beyond his control make this difficult: for instance on windy days when teaching outside, his voice may not carry well despite his best efforts, and on such occasions a microphone may be invaluable. When teaching for prolonged periods, it is advisable for the instructor to keep a drink of water on hand to combat problems caused by a dry throat. Dusty conditions should either be avoided, or controlled, if that is possible, by (for example) sprinkling the riding arena. This would be in the interests of the health and wellbeing of the horses and riders, as well as for the benefit of the instructor's voice.

The instructor's words need to carry well, and be comprehensible at all times. Sometimes regional accents or dialects can cause pupils to mishear or misunderstand. In this case the instructor may need to make an effort to tone down regional variations and to enunciate his words clearly.

Difficulties in communication can also arise if a pupil suffers from defective hearing. Hopefully the instructor will be apprised of such problems before a lesson commences, but it may be as well for him to enquire early in the lesson if everyone can hear him.

Terminology

Terminology in common equestrian usage is often employed loosely, and can be ambiguous in meaning. If the instructor feels it is necessary for technical terms or phrases to be used, he should clarify them first with a clear, concise explanation or description in order to avoid future misinterpretation or confusion. The teacher should also remember that beginners and novice pupils will be unfamiliar with many of the simpler words and phrases in everyday equestrian use, and may be baffled by some of the directions given unless they have first been fully explained.

Verbal skills

A good instructor will be able to use his voice to great effect, and to adapt his tone of voice to suit the characteristics of the pupil's mount, the pupil and his level of ability.

Through variation of pitch, tone and volume he can:

- convey enthusiasm;
- inspire the pupil to greater efforts;
- promote confidence and trust;
- be calming and reassuring;
- make the pupil feel important, and his custom valued;
- keep the pupil's attention, and also gain that of the horse if necessary.

The instructor should constantly try to refine and improve his verbal skills and powers of description, and it is vital that he base them upon his own experience and observations, rather than merely repeating parrot-fashion the comments of others. He should be flexible and imaginative enough to be able to re-word phrases or explanations, when necessary, in such a way that the pupil can grasp a concept.

The teacher must always allow the pupil sufficient time to absorb and act upon one instruction or comment, before he follows it with another. The pupil is unlikely to cope if he is asked to perform too many actions simultaneously.

COMMON FAULTS

- **Shouting:** This sounds aggressive and intimidating, and if others are teaching in the school at the same time, it can drown them out. It is also a strain on the voice.
- **Too quiet:** A very quiet delivery is frequently due to an instructor lacking confidence in himself, but it may also be due to nervousness, or to poor posture.
- **A high-pitched voice:** This may be natural to the individual, but it can stem from nervousness, or it may be an incorrect attempt to project the voice. It is often harsh and grating for the pupil to listen to.
- **A droning, monotonous voice:** This is boring for the pupil to listen to, with the result that his attention often wanders. It also implies that the instructor is not particularly interested in the pupil, and betrays a lack of enthusiasm.
- **Speaking too fast:** A hurried delivery may be due to an underlying lack of confidence, impatience with a pupil, or over-eagerness in trying to get a point or idea across. Over-rapid speech makes it difficult for the pupil to assimilate all the information, and words may tend to run together.

PART SIX: Types of

Lesson

Private and Group Lessons

✔ An excellent teacher can keep his pupils spellbound.
✔ All exercises performed on one rein should be repeated on the other one.

Lessons may be divided into three categories: private, semi-private and group instruction. The duration of lessons will vary accordingly.

Private lessons

Private lessons are conducted on a one-to-one basis, and include lead-rein and lunge lessons as well as pupils capable of riding independently. All beginners should receive private tuition until such time as they are considered ready to join a group lesson.

Private lessons may also be of greater benefit to more advanced pupils than a class lesson if they either have their own horse, or wish to compete, or to concentrate on a particular problem they have been encountering, since the instruction can be more specifically tailored to meet their particular requirements.

Semi-private lessons

Semi-private lessons – that is, comprising two riders – enable pupils to enjoy many of the benefits of private lessons at a slightly cheaper rate. They might also be employed as an intermediate step for those who have progressed from the lead rein to riding independently, prior to joining a group lesson. To be of benefit, both pupils should be at a similar standard.

Group lessons

Before joining a group lesson, pupils should be riding independently of the lead rein and should be able to manage the following procedures:

- Check and adjust the tightness of the girth, both prior to, and whilst mounted.
- Place the reins correctly over the horse's head and neck.
- Mount and dismount unaided.
- Lengthen and shorten the stirrup leathers unaided prior to, and whilst mounted.
- Understand the basic principles of correct posture, and the aids for asking the horse to move forwards, halt and turn.
- Halt, walk, and manage at least one complete circuit of the school in trot, both sitting and rising.
- Ride simple changes of direction in walk.

DURATION OF LESSONS Due to the more intense aspect of private instruction, 30 minutes is usually quite sufficient for beginners who are unaccustomed to the physical demands of riding, although more advanced riders may be able to cope with longer periods of between 45 minutes to one hour. Group lessons may range from half to one hour in duration, depending upon the ability and age of the pupil: some younger children may not be able to sustain concentration, nor do they possess the physical stamina to cope with more than half an hour, for example.

Riders in group lessons should be of a similar level of ability so that all pupils benefit equally from instruction. This is of greater importance than grouping by age, although where possible, adults and children should be taught separately.

When teaching very novice groups, it may be helpful to have an experienced and competent rider available, mounted on a sensible and steady horse, to act as leading file. If pupils have recently graduated to a group from lead-rein lessons, one or more dismounted assistants should be on hand – whether a leading file is present or not – to assist when necessary.

The dimensions of the school will dictate to some extent the number of riders participating in each group lesson. In schools of 20m x 40m, the maximum number of pupils should be around eight, in order to ensure both safety and quality of instruction. In smaller areas than this, the number of pupils will need to be reduced accordingly. Where very novice groups are concerned, it is best if they are limited to three or four in number until a greater degree of proficiency has been gained.

Simultaneous lessons

The number of lessons which can be conducted simultaneously in the school depends on its size, and the type of instruction being given:

- Where the dimensions of the school are 20m x 40m or greater, and it can be safely and effectively divided, two group lessons may be taught at the same time, provided there are no more than four pupils in each, and neither group is being given jumping instruction. It should be appreciated however, that this will necessarily limit the variety of school movements which may be ridden, and the teacher should take care to ensure that whilst his own pupils can hear him clearly, he does not drown out his colleague.

■ If a lunge lesson is taking place in the school at the same time as group or private lessons, the school should first be divided by a barrier of some kind.

■ Where the school is divided, no more than either two

lead-rein lessons, one small group, one semi-private, or one lunge lesson should take place in each half.

■ If no group or lunge lessons are taking place, it may be possible to conduct four to six individual lead-rein lessons in a school with dimensions of 20m x 40m or greater.

■ When a group lesson is taking place using the entire area of the school, no lead-rein lessons should be given.

■ Private lessons should not be conducted whilst jumping lessons are taking place in the same area.

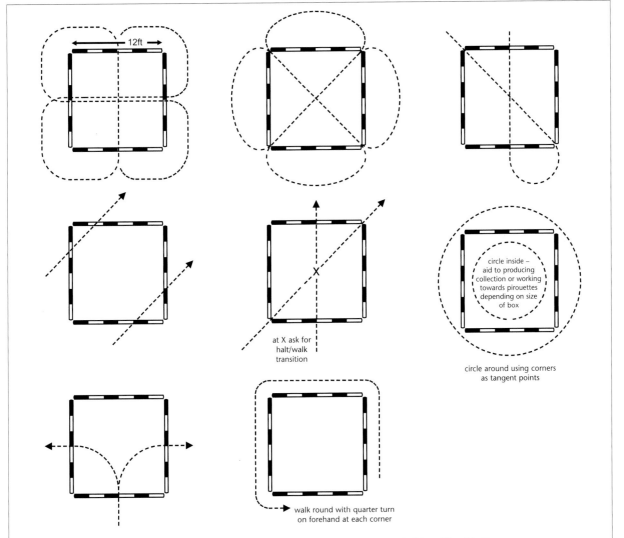

When performing box exercises for bigger/stiffer horses you can use eight poles instead of four. The objectives are accuracy, activity, suppleness and obedience. The exercises are useful for pre-course riding and warming up for jumping, or for variety in flatwork. They are also good for developing horse and rider concentration and improving reflexes, quick thinking and co-ordination. Using box exercises with horses which rush may be more successful than with single/lines of poles, which may excite them. The constant turning also helps to encourage balance and steadiness. Vary the exercises to avoid anticipation. They can all be ridden at walk and trot unless otherwise indicated on the diagrams.

Lead-rein Lessons

✔ Do not simply instruct the pupil on *how* something should be done – explain *why*. If he understands the underlying reasoning for taking a certain action it will make more sense to him, and he will be far more likely to remember it.

Lessons on the lead rein enable the teacher to ensure that the horse remains under close control whilst he teaches a beginner or a nervous rider the basics of position and the aids for stopping, starting and turning. The close proximity of the teacher, as well as the fact that he is holding the horse, both help to instil confidence in the pupil, especially if he is at all anxious.

Attaching and holding the lead rein

The lead rein should ideally be clipped to a bit coupling. If one is not available, when leading from the near (left) side of the horse, the lead rein should be slipped through the near-side bit-ring, beneath the lower jaw, and clipped to the off-side bit-ring. When leading from the off (right) side of the horse, this should be reversed, removing the lead rein and re-attaching it by slipping it through the off-side bit-ring, beneath the lower jaw and clipping it onto the near-side bit-ring. The lead rein should never be attached solely to the bit-ring closest to the teacher, as this gives less control and may cause the bit to be pulled through the side of the horse's mouth.

When changing direction, the teacher should change the side he is leading from, so that he is on the inner side of the horse, i.e., closest to the centre of the school, where he does not risk becoming crushed between the horse and the school walls. This is most safely achieved by first halting the horse, when alterations to the attachment of the lead rein may be made if necessary; he should not move directly in front of the horse whilst it is still in movement.

A correctly held web lead rein

Lead-rein Lessons

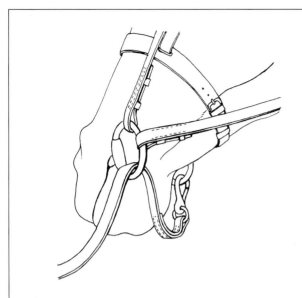

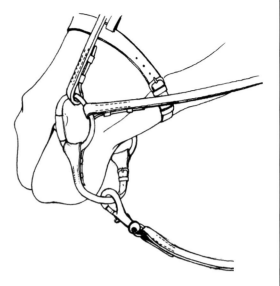

The correct way of attaching a lead rein to the bit when taking a lead rein lesson – leading from the near (left) side of horse. This should be reversed when leading from the off (right) side

If available, bit coupling eliminates the need to change the lead rein over when leading from the other side

The teacher should wear gloves, and keep the end of the lead rein and any excess length coiled neatly in the hand furthest away from the horse, so that it does not become a hazard dragging along the ground. The hand closest to the horse should hold the lead rein at a distance of around 12–18in (30–45cm) away from the bit. The lead rein must not be wrapped tightly around the hand, and the end should never be flicked at the horse's side as a means of encouraging forward movement: such an action may startle or frighten even a generally placid horse, causing it to rush forwards or shy sideways, when it could easily alarm, unbalance and/or possibly unseat the pupil.

Lesson content

Bearing in mind that the pupil has an overwhelmingly large amount of information to absorb and remember during his first lessons, the teacher should not become irritable or impatient if he has to repeat instructions or corrections. Even during successive lessons this may be the case: a degree of competence or knowledge should not be assumed just because he has already told his pupil something once already.

During his first lessons, the pupil should be taught the following:

- Where to go to collect his horse and how to lead it to the school under strict supervision.
- How to check the tightness of the girth and place the reins correctly over the horse's head and neck.

- How to mount and dismount.
- How to check and adjust the tightness of the girth whilst mounted.
- How to ascertain the correct length of stirrup and adjust them as necessary before and after mounting.
- How to hold the reins in one and/or both hands.
- The correct posture in the saddle.
- The aids for stopping, starting and turning.
- The rules of the school.

Even during these earliest stages of tuition, the teacher should encourage the pupil's perception or 'feel' for how the horse stands, moves and responds to his aids: initially this may be in a limited way, and the teacher will need to inform him as to when and why a certain action might be considered correct or incorrect, and suggest how the effort might be improved.

Encouragement is the most important and vital element of instruction, but especially so at this stage when lack of experience, knowledge, suppleness and co-ordination may cause the pupil a certain amount of frustration. Praise should always be forthcoming for an improved effort, even if it falls far short of the ideal which pupil and teacher are striving for.

Progression

Lead-rein instruction is generally conducted on a one-to-one basis during a pupil's first two or three lessons.

Depending upon the aptitude of the pupil, the facilities, and the number of staff available to assist, further lessons may then progress as follows:

- **As a small group**: A qualified member of staff or trainee instructor must be available to lead each pupil's horse until such time as they are ready to engage in independent work.
- **Lunge work**: The pupil continues with tuition on a one-to-one basis, but moves from the lead rein to the lunge rein, where he can further develop his posture and aid application, and work for slightly more extended periods in trot, until such time as he is ready to join a group lesson.
- **Independent work**: The pupil continues with tuition on a one-to-one basis: when the teacher feels he is ready, the lead rein is removed and he begins to work independently – unless riding on the lunge commences – until his control is such that he can safely join a group lesson.

Beginning work off the lead/lunge rein

The transition from work on the lead rein and/or lunge rein to independent work should be made gradually. When the pupil is able to accomplish certain movements without the teacher having to encourage/guide the horse – namely transitions between halt, walk and trot, simple changes of direction in walk, and the ability to confidently trot short distances – the lead rein can be removed. The teacher should remain by the side of the horse at first because the rider will draw confidence from his continued close presence; he will also then be able to step in quickly to assist should the rider encounter difficulties, or if his readiness for this stage has been misjudged.

Some riders may be very self-assured whilst on the lead rein, but can become apprehensive and anxious when first released from it: only when the teacher is sure of the pupil's confidence and ability to maintain control should he gradually begin to move further away from the horse's side.

PRECAUTIONS Horses used for lead-rein lessons must be steady and calm in temperament, they should lead freely from both sides, and should not be inclined to habits such as biting at the teacher's hand or the lead rein, or to displays of temper or aggression towards other horses which may be present in the school. Ideally the horse should also be smooth and comfortable in its action, forward-going but without any tendency to excitability, and responsive to the pupil's aids but unlikely to become alarmed by any exercises he may perform, or inadvertent movements he may make.

The teacher should at all times be aware of other riders who are in the school at the same time so as to avoid placing either them, himself, his pupil or the horse in a potentially dangerous situation. He should also appreciate the fact that the pupil may initially find the movement of the horse alarming and unbalancing, and should encourage him to make use of the neckstrap when necessary. Avoid asking the horse for a more active gait until the rider is first accustomed to the unfamiliar motion.

Lunge Work for the Rider

✔ Always warn the pupil in advance before asking the horse to make an upward or downward transition.

✔ Take great care in handling the lunge whip, as an abrupt movement with it may cause the horse to shy or suddenly rush forwards, unbalancing and possibly unseating the rider. The whip should be used sensibly to indicate to the horse what is required, never as a threat.

Correct work on the lunge is an excellent way of helping pupils at all levels, from novice to advanced, provided it is safely and knowledgeably managed by an experienced and skilled teacher.

Benefits

Correct lunge work may be used to help the pupil:

■ establish, or further refine, a secure, comfortable and correct posture in the saddle;

■ improve his balance, suppleness, co-ordination and aid application.

Work on the lunge allows the pupil to concentrate to a greater extent on himself because he doesn't have to control and direct the horse as well. This enables him to perform a wide variety of stretching and suppling exercises, both with and without reins and stirrups, that are not normally possible when riding off the lunge.

In the case of a novice rider who has achieved a degree of confidence on the leading rein in walk, the teacher is able to progress to teaching him work in trot with ease and safety, and to further prepare him for riding independently.

Intelligently tackled by the teacher, this early lunge work will provide the pupil with a firm foundation for all his future riding activities, and in addition will instil a sense of confidence.

Teacher skills

Before ever attempting to give a lunge lesson, the teacher must first have achieved a high degree of competence in lungeing an unmounted horse, and in handling the equipment. He must also possess a sound knowledge of rider posture, and should have tried the horse out before placing a pupil in the saddle.

It is also advantageous if he has received instruction on the lunge himself, as this will greatly enhance his own understanding of this type of instruction, and increase his ability to assist the pupil.

Preparing the horse

The lunge horse should be given the chance to loosen off for a few minutes on both reins before the pupil mounts. This brief period also ensures that the horse is settled and obedient to the teacher's commands before the lesson starts. Until

THE LUNGE HORSE

Horses used for lunge lessons must be suitable for the purpose if instruction is to be both constructive and safe. It is essential that they are:

■ reliable, steady and sensible in temperament;
■ reasonably free moving, but without excitability;
■ obedient;
■ well balanced with correct, regular and rhythmical gaits;
■ fit enough for the work;
■ familiar with ridden lunge work.

The bridle reins should be secured as shown here whilst lungeing the horse without a rider

the rider is ready to mount, the bridle reins should be twisted around each other and the throatlash threaded through them and secured again, so they do not dangle dangerously low around the horse's front legs. The stirrup irons must be run up the leathers and secured in such a fashion that they cannot slip down.

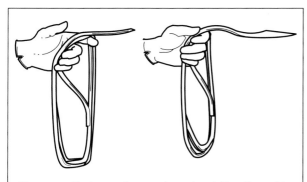

Never wrap the lunge rein around your hand. Keep the end in a loop with the thumb placed uppermost on top of the rein

Mounting and dismounting the rider

Before the rider mounts the horse, the teacher should ascertain whether he has previously received any tuition on the lunge: if not, he should first explain a little about how it can be of benefit, and what will happen during the course of the lesson.

Once the tack has been checked, the reins freed from the throatlash and the stirrups run down the leathers, the pupil may be assisted to mount, and the lesson can commence. Whenever the pupil is mounting/dismounting, or adjusting stirrups or girth, the side reins must always be detached from the bridle bit-rings and clipped to the metal D-rings on the front of the saddle.

Centrifugal force

The teacher should be aware of the effect of centrifugal force on the pupil whilst working on the lunge circle; this will increase with gait speed, and also if the circle is allowed to become too small. Despite the pupil's best efforts to follow the teacher's advice, it may cause his seat to slip towards the outside, making it difficult for him to maintain

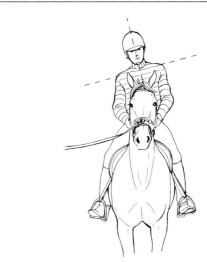

INCORRECT The teacher should check the pupil's straightness from in front when halting to change the rein, as well as in profile. There may be a tendency for the rider to lean inwards or twist on a circle Remember a striped top can cause optical illusions!

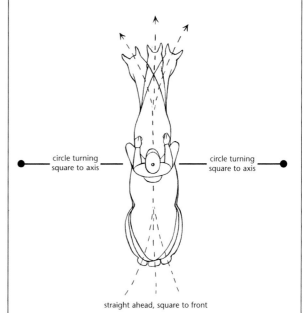

Work on the circle is demanding for the horse and can cause postural difficulties for the rider. He should be encouraged to remain square to axis and not lean/twist his body in an effort to counter centrifugal force

Lunge Work for the Rider

his position and security, and for the horse to remain balanced. When this is observed, the teacher should if necessary walk, or even halt the horse to allow the pupil to correct his position and regain his balance.

Changes of direction
The teacher should change the direction at least twice on each rein during the lesson in order to observe both sides of the rider, and to prevent any tendency of either pupil or horse to favour one rein more than the other. This will also

allow horse and rider a brief moment of rest, and if the teacher feels it to be beneficial at that point, the opportunity for discussion. Each time a change of rein is made, the teacher should always check the pupil's straightness.

Work with and without reins and stirrups
When the reins are held by the rider, the contact with the horse's mouth should be minimal, and should not contradict the action of the side reins. If the rider is

working without reins, they should be knotted at the buckle end and allowed to lie on the horse's neck: on these occasions the teacher should keep an eye on them to ensure they do not slide along/down the horse's neck if he lowers his head.

When the rider is working without stirrups, the buckles of the leathers should be pulled away from the stirrup bars by a few inches, and the leathers and irons then crossed over the horse's neck in front of the saddle. The buckles will not then form an uncomfortable bulge under the rider's thighs, and the irons will not bump against either the horse's sides or the rider's ankles.

When teaching a very novice or nervous pupil it may be advisable to allow him to retain his reins and stirrups until balance/posture is stabilised and secure.

Intelligently handled, lungework can benefit riders of all abilities, allowing them to concentrate on their own position and their teacher's instruction

Top right: Pulling the buckle of the stirrup leathers away from the stirrup bars before crossing them will ensure the rider is more comfortable when working without stirrups

Right: Attaching side reins to girth straps

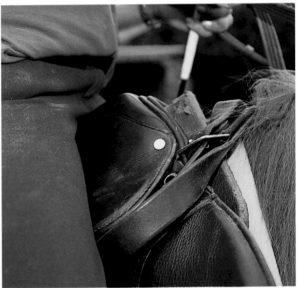

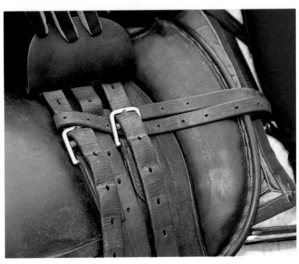

Dismounted Exercises

✔ Select exercises with a specific objective in mind, not merely for the sake of giving the pupil something to do.

✔ Remember that your aim is to create a rider with integrated posture and co-ordination: try to avoid viewing him simply as a series of unrelated anatomical parts.

Pupils may also profit from exercises which can be performed on the ground, particularly if they are unable to ride on a daily basis. These can assist in developing and maintaining suppleness, flexibility and co-ordination between lessons, and may also be used as a form of gentle warm up immediately prior to riding.

(1) Allow the head to tilt forward slightly and slowly draw a figure of infinity sign (∞) in the air with the nose. This will help release tension in the neck and jaw.

(2 & 3) Shrug both shoulders upwards and then allow them to roll backwards and downwards again to help loosen tense, stiff shoulders.

(4) With feet spaced comfortably apart and a hand placed on each hip, slowly rotate the upper body from left to right and then from right to left to help supple the waist area.

(5 & 6) *Slowly circle each arm in turn to relax tense, stiff shoulders and encourage a better posture through the trunk.*

(7 & 8) *With fingertips lightly touching the top of the shoulder, draw a circle in the air with the elbow. If the shoulders are very stiff, start with smaller circles, gradually enlarging them.*

(9) *Place one foot on a chair, using a hand on the back of it to assist in balance if necessary. Slowly lean forwards over the raised knee, keeping the heel of the opposite foot flat on the ground. The exercise should then be repeated, switching over the positions of the legs. This exercise can be a great help to pupils who tend to find mounting difficult or who ride with the heels drawing upwards, but should not be forced to the point where extreme discomfort is felt.*

Dismounted Exercises

(1 & 2) *Another waist-suppling exercise, helpful for pupils who tend to collapse through one hip. The pupil should be encouraged to stretch to an equal degree to each side.*

(3, 4 & 5) *Further suppleness can be achieved through use of this exercise. Both arms should be maintained at the same height as the pupil turns from side to side.*

(6 & 7) *For this exercise, the pupil stands just far enough away from a wall so that the palms of both hands can be rested flat against it. Bending both elbows, the pupil allows the body to incline forwards at an angle to the ground. Both heels should be kept flat on the floor. This exercise helps to stretch the calf muscle, but should not be forced.*

(8 & 9) *With arms just below shoulder height and elbows bent so that the fingertips just meet, the elbows are slowly pushed backwards, moving the hands apart. This is helpful for those who tend to round their shoulders and collapse forwards when riding.*

Mounted Exercises

✔ The instructor should endeavour to have regular lessons himself, as this provides a greater appreciation of the benefits, demands and difficulties of each horse's gaits and of the various exercises.

✔ Avoid overtiring the rider.

Stretching and suppling exercises may be used to help the pupil generally settle in at the beginning of a lesson; they may also help him overcome specific postural problems later on during the course of instruction. Pupils may perform beneficial exercises on the lead rein, lunge rein, or during independent ridden work. Some exercises aim to develop suppleness, improve co-ordination, promote the independent use of the limbs and reduce tension; others help to strengthen his muscles, improve his balance and increase his confidence.

Considerations

When using exercises, the teacher should:

- Take into account the individual pupil's physique, and any history of physical problems which may affect his ability to perform a particular exercise.
- Avoid over-frequent repetitions or excessive movement, as this may cause cramping or strain of the muscles, and can distort the rest of the posture.
- Explain each exercise carefully, and ensure the pupil understands what is required.
- Explain the benefit of the exercise, relating it to any particular problems a pupil might have.
- Perform all exercises correctly on both reins.
- Allow the pupil a brief rest period between each exercise, or alternate easier exercises with more demanding ones: overtiring the rider will lead to incorrect, insecure and unsafe posture.

Safety

Great care must always be taken when asking pupils to perform any exercises:

- Novice or nervous pupils should not be asked to work without stirrups until balance and posture are stabilised.
- Gait speed should not be increased beyond that with which the pupil can cope.
- When teaching group lessons, the teacher should ask each pupil in turn to perform the exercise, rather than all the pupils at the same time.
- The pupil should not be asked to do exercises on a horse which is liable to become upset by his movements.
- Encourage the pupil to perform each exercise slowly and smoothly: this will be more beneficial to him, it will enable him to remain balanced, and is less likely to lead to strains or to disturb the horse.

The exercises illustrated overleaf are the most fundamental and useful, but are just a basic core. Those exercises which require the rider to release both reins simultaneously are suitable only for lead-rein or lunge lessons, but may be modified to allow a pupil riding independently to perform them if he takes both reins into one hand, leaving the other free to execute the exercise. In this instance, the teacher should first show the pupil how to hold the reins correctly in one hand.

Mounted Exercises

(1) *With the head tilted slightly forward, draw a figure of infinity sign (∞) in the air with the nose to release tension in the neck and jaw.*

(2 & 3) *Shrug both shoulders upwards towards the ears and then allow them to ease downwards to loosen tense, stiff shoulders.*

(4) *Arms folded behind back to correct body posture.*

(5) *With arms at shoulder height and elbows flexed so fingertips just touch, push the elbows backwards slowly, moving the hands apart. This is helpful for those who tend to round their shoulders and/or collapse forwards through the ribcage when riding.*

(6) *Circle each extended arm in turn, forwards, upwards and backwards to avoid a round-shouldered posture.*

(7) *Encouraging the pupil to stretch upwards with both hands to develop upright body posture.*

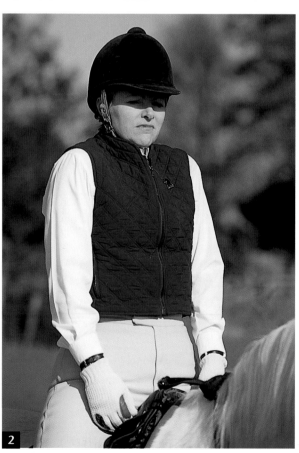

Mounted Exercises

(1 & 2) *Stretch arms out to each side, slowly turning to the left then right to promote waist suppleness.*

(3) *Riding with the palm of the hand on the abdomen and the back of the other hand on the lower back indicates the area where the rider absorbs the horse's movement with the seat.*

(4) *Open hands placed over the pelvis in the small of the waist allows the rider to press the buttocks onto the saddle, and so deepen the seat.*

(5) *Performed only in halt or slow walk, touching opposite toes can be useful in building confidence, suppleness, balance and co-ordination.*

(6) *Circling the toes of each foot clockwise and anti-clockwise, slowly turning, will help supple stiff ankle joints.*

Jumping Lessons

✔ Teach what you understand.

✔ Encourage pupils not to compete with others but to compete with themselves.

Jumping instruction can be an enjoyable activity for both pupils and horses, but correct and sensible management by the riding teacher is vital for the safety and welfare of all participants, equine as well as human.

The jumping horse

Horses used for the purposes of jumping instruction should be suitable for the task. They should be sensible and calm, but reasonably free-going: whilst a horse which is inclined to be sluggish may promote confidence in a nervous rider, if it approaches fences in a similar fashion it will invariably jump awkwardly, making it difficult for the rider to remain in a balanced and secure position.

The teacher should remember that although jumping is generally fun for riders, it is a strenuous and demanding activity for the horse, so rest periods are essential, particularly if it is taking part in other lessons during the day.

Warming up

Before tackling any obstacles, both horse and rider must first have been given ample opportunity to warm up. This serves several purposes:

■ it enables the pupil to loosen off;

■ it reduces the risk of injury or strain to the horse;

■ it allows the pupil sufficient time to become familiar with the horse he is riding;

■ it ensures that the horse is attentive and obedient to the rider's aids.

Preparatory work for jumping should include walk, trot and canter on both reins, and the inclusion of exercises such as transitions, circles and changes of direction.

Polework

Polework may be used as a complete lesson in itself, as an introduction to jumping for novice pupils, or as part of the warm-up work before greater jumping effort for more proficient and experienced pupils. An imaginative instructor will be able to devise many variations on polework exercises to ensure that neither horse nor rider becomes bored. When teaching pupils or horses which are an unknown quantity, the introduction of simple polework exercises prior to building a small fence will assist the instructor in gauging the competence and attitude of both.

Polework can form a useful introduction to jumping for the novice rider. Distances should be kept to a comfortable distance for the horse

(Right) Polework can be used to help improve horse/rider skills on the flat and as preparation for jumping lessons. It also improves rhythm and balance, restores correct locomotion/movement, increases impulsion and teaches stride shortening and lengthening

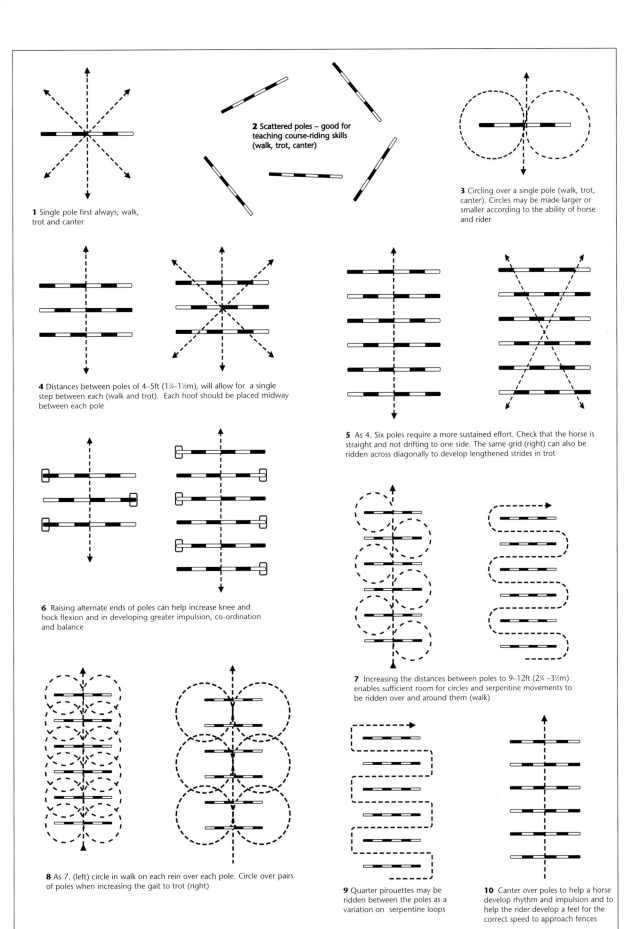

1 Single pole first always; walk, trot and canter

2 Scattered poles – good for teaching course-riding skills (walk, trot, canter)

3 Circling over a single pole (walk, trot, canter). Circles may be made larger or smaller according to the ability of horse and rider

4 Distances between poles of 4–5ft (1¼–1½m), will allow for a single step between each (walk and trot). Each hoof should be placed midway between each pole

5 As 4. Six poles require a more sustained effort. Check that the horse is straight and not drifting to one side. The same grid (right) can also be ridden across diagonally to develop lengthened strides in trot

6 Raising alternate ends of poles can help increase knee and hock flexion and in developing greater impulsion, co-ordination and balance

7 Increasing the distances between poles to 9–12ft (2¾ –3½m) enables sufficient room for circles and serpentine movements to be ridden over and around them (walk)

8 As 7. (left) circle in walk on each rein over each pole. Circle over pairs of poles when increasing the gait to trot (right)

9 Quarter pirouettes may be ridden between the poles as a variation on serpentine loops

10 Canter over poles to help a horse develop rhythm and impulsion and to help the rider develop a feel for the correct speed to approach fences

Jumping Lessons

Teaching novice pupils

When instructing novice pupils, once they have completed their initial warm-up, the teacher should spend a little time discussing the theory of jumping, including the importance of accuracy of approach, establishing and maintaining rhythm and impulsion, and the correct position for the rider. This may be accompanied by a demonstration, if he feels this is appropriate; and then the pupil can attempt to put it all into practice. The lesson should therefore progress as follows:

- stirrup leathers shortened by two to three holes from the flatwork length;
- practise of the jumping position whilst in halt;
- work on the flat in walk, trot and canter to allow the pupil to become accustomed to a shorter length of stirrup whilst the horse is in motion;
- work over a single pole in walk and trot;
- adoption of the jumping position as the horse moves over the poles in trot.

Once the pupil is secure and confident, and shows himself to be competent in these exercises, a small fence can be

Use of a correctly positioned placing pole in front of a fence can ensure that the horse takes off from the optimum place to give a safe and comfortable jump for the rider

introduced. A low crosspole is to be preferred, as this will encourage both horse and rider to approach straight and to jump the central, lowest part of the obstacle, thus establishing good habits for the future. The height of the poles where they cross may be varied according to the size of the horse: it should be just high enough to give the pupil the sensation of the horse leaving the ground, but not so high that the effort it produces is unseating.

A placing pole should be laid on the ground on the approach side of the fence at a distance of between 8–9ft (2.4–2.7m) from the base of the obstacle, depending on the size of the horse. This ensures that the horse will meet the fence at a correct take-off point, thereby further reducing the likelihood of an over-extravagant or clumsy effort in order to clear it, which would make it difficult for an inexperienced pupil to remain in balance. The placing pole also fulfills a further function in that it enables the pupil to anticipate and begin to judge the point at which the horse will take off, so that it does not catch him unawares.

Initially this work should take place in trot, as the pupil will gain confidence from being in a slower gait. Only when he is confident and secure jumping small fences from trot should he be asked to approach in canter.

(Left) Simple grids of fences can be fun for both horse and rider as well as encouraging a forward going and correct style in both

(Below) Examples of progressive gridwork exercises

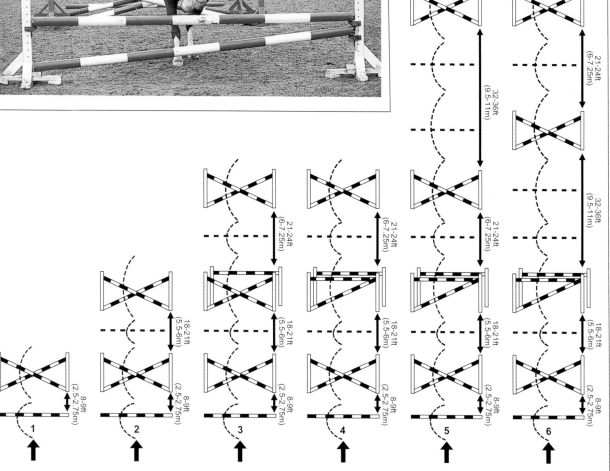

Gridwork exercises should be built up progressively and according to the horse/rider's ability. The teacher should never try to trap the horse but rather try to educate it through the use of grids.

1 A simple warm-up fence, approaching in trot and enabling the teacher to assess horse/rider abilities.

2 Approaching in trot and landing in canter after the first fence. The teacher should remember that when approaching a fence in trot, the length of stride on landing will be slightly shorter than if the approach is in canter. Jumping out of trot encourages a more athletic effort without having to build higher fences.

3 The second fence is built into an ascending spread and a third fence introduced.

4 The second fence is changed to a square parallel to encourage the horse to use himself more fully. Note that the first and last fences are cross poles, to encourage straightness through the grid.

5 Introducing a fourth fence, two non-jumping strides away from the third fence, will encourage a slightly stuffy horse to go forward and help maintain impulsion.

6 The exercise can be varied by leaving two non-jumping strides between the second and third fences, and one non-jumping stride between the third and fourth fences. The last two fences will encourage the horse to engage its hocks and lighten its forehand and to think more quickly.

Jumping Lessons

Cross-country lessons

Particular care must be taken when giving cross-country lessons, both because of the solid and unforgiving nature of the obstacles themselves, and because horses may become more excitable than when show-jumping. Pupils participating in cross-country instruction should be of Intermediate level or above. The teacher should prepare them for this work by instructing them on riding technique over varying terrains and gradients, and before they tackle different types of obstacle, should brief them on the appropriate manner of approach.

It is strongly recommended that pupils should wear a body protector for cross-country instruction.

Safety

Fences must be built of suitable materials, and constructed in such a way as to be safe and inviting (see Jumping Equipment, page 31). The teacher should proceed within the following parameters:

- The height and width of fences must always be kept within the horse and rider's ability to cope.
- When setting up poles, or combinations of fences for class lessons, the distances between each must be compatible for the whole group.
- Less experienced pupils should be encouraged to make use of a neckstrap or to hold the mane for additional security, and to save the horse from being repeatedly jabbed in the mouth.
- In group lessons, care must be taken to position the rest of the ride safely away from fences whilst each pupil is jumping, in order to avoid accidents.
- Pupils should not be asked to work as a ride over fences, as this may lead to horses becoming excitable or injuries occurring if a rider becomes unseated or a horse stops unexpectedly.
- The teacher should never chase a horse forwards over a fence.
- When jumping outdoors, horses may be more inclined to become excitable, and the teacher should be vigilant for signs of this. He should also be prepared to adapt his lesson to take into account the prevailing ground and weather conditions (see Riding Outdoors, page 28).

Pupils taking cross-country lessons should be adequately briefed by the teacher as to the appropriate way to tackle each type of fence before being asked to jump them

MORE ADVANCED RIDERS

More advanced pupils may be set more demanding exercises according to their ability and that of the horse, including:

- the introduction of obstacles that vary in height, width, shape and appearance;
- simple combinations of fences;
- courses of fences;
- gridwork and gymnastic exercises.

When instructing more advanced pupils, the teacher should not be tempted to hurry horse and pupil through the early warming-up phases of the lesson. Even though the pupil may be (or profess to be) very competent, the first fences which he jumps should be kept simple and low, and the height/width/complexity of exercise built up in a gradual and logical progression to avoid the risk of injury or loss of confidence through overfacing either horse or rider.

Hacking Out

✔ Do not allow clients to ride with their feet out of the stirrups whilst hacking.

✔ Do not allow slower horses at the rear of the ride to get left so far behind that they lose sight of the other horses.

✔ Always return to the yard in walk, with the horses cool, dry and relaxed.

Hacking out can have many benefits for the pupil: in controlling his mount over different terrain and surroundings he will learn how to use skills acquired in the school; hacking introduces welcome variety from formal instruction for both horse and rider; and it offers pupils the opportunity to enjoy the countryside from horseback.

Clothing and equipment

- The clothing of both pupils and escorts must be suitable for riding. Escorts at the front and rear of the ride should also wear a high visibility tabard.
- All horses should ideally wear neckstraps or breastplates which pupils should be encouraged to hold if they become unbalanced.

In addition, the escort in charge of the ride should carry:

- Pocket first aid kit.
- Leading rein.
- Folding hoofpick.
- Notebook and safe writing instrument.
- Map of intended route if necessary.
- Mobile phone if possible or money/telephone card. Although calls to the emergency services are free from public telephone boxes, the escort may find himself in a situation which does not constitute an emergency as such, but does necessitate making a call to the yard.
- Any appropriate licence discs for riding in particular areas where a fee is levied for doing so by the landowner.
- Length of twine for emergency repairs.
- A whistle when riding in areas which are isolated, or where rescuers may find it difficult to spot the ride; it may be blown to attract attention.

A group of pupils, mounted and preparing to hack out as a group

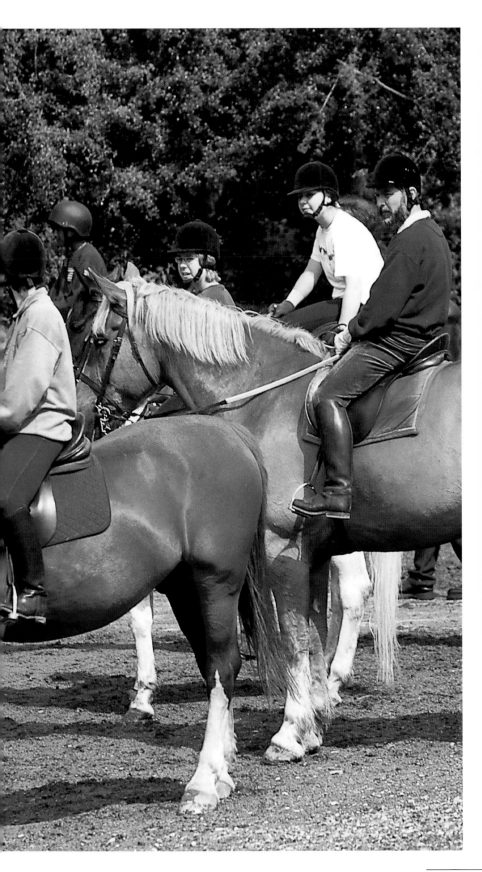

ESCORTS It is suggested that when hacking out the group should not exceed more than eight pupils in number. With groups of four or more pupils, at least one assistant escort should accompany the hack leader to act as rear file, to ensure that no one gets into difficulties or is left behind, and to give hand signals when appropriate. This is particularly important on winding tracks or in leafy woodland areas, where the hack leader may not always have clear visibility of those riders towards the rear, and on roads, when motorists may not always be able to see the hack leader's hand signals.

At least one escort should hold 'Riding & Road Safety' and first-aid qualifications, whilst other escorts must be a minimum of sixteen years of age, and sufficiently competent and experienced to act in this capacity.

Hacking Out

Horses

As with formal riding instruction, the pupil should be allocated a horse which is suitable in size, temperament and behaviour for his experience and ability. Horses ridden by escorts must not be nappy or difficult to control, but should be calm and sensible enough that the rider can:

- maintain ride control;
- take up a variety of positions within the ride and halt them when necessary in order to assist pupils;
- direct traffic when required;
- mount again with ease should it be necessary for him to dismount for some reason;
- safely mount a pupil on an escort horse should the pupil's horse go lame.

In addition, all the horses must be sound, fit enough, and sufficiently well schooled and well balanced to cope with the demands of the terrain and the duration and speed of the hack.

The escort should not miss any opportunity out hacking to further a rider's education, whether it be riding over varying terrain or putting skills learnt in the school into practical use – opening and shutting gates for example, using turn on the forehand

Route

The hack escort should know the route he is planning to take sufficiently well that he:

- does not become lost;
- can avoid dangerous going and forewarn the ride of any hazards ahead;
- can accurately assess the speed at which he needs to go in order to return home on time.

Before leaving the yard he should inform a responsible member of staff of the precise route he intends to take, and he should remain on it. He should also be familiar with the names of the fields, roads and landmarks along the way, so that were an accident to occur, help might be summoned to the right place, and with any necessary specialist vehicles in the event of difficult terrain.

Weather conditions

- Local weather forecasts should be checked before going out, especially in areas where mists may fall quickly and with little warning.
- Pupils should not be taken out hacking in conditions of poor visibility – for example, mist, fog, driving rain, or when the light is failing.

- Caution should be taken if rain has fallen, as this may cause slippery and treacherous going.
- Hacking out should not be contemplated in icy conditions.
- Cold/wet/windy weather may cause horses to behave skittishly, especially if they have been clipped. Some horses may also be frightened and inclined to shy if windy conditions cause stray paper or plastic bags or other pieces of discarded rubbish to be blown around.
- Consideration for the welfare of the horses should be exercised in hot weather, and when the ground is hard.

Ride organisation

The hack escort should place horses in a sensible order, with larger, longer-striding or more free-moving animals at the front, and those which are smaller/shorter-striding towards the rear. Before setting out he should carry out the same safety checks as when taking a lesson (see Saddlery, Clothing, and Safety). He should also brief the ride on the distances to be kept between horses, and on how to prevent difficult situations from arising – such as might occur from allowing horses to graze, for example.

During the hack, he should check behind him frequently to ensure that he is setting a suitable speed, and that none of the riders is experiencing difficulties. Warning of changes in gait, difficult terrain, or hazards such as low-hanging branches, should be given in plenty of time, and if necessary the ride should be halted so that advice and instruction may be given as to how to deal with such eventualities.

Hacking should be an enjoyable activity for pupils, and the hack escort should encourage this aspect. In trot or when cantering, the ride should be kept in single file, but whilst in walk, if off-road tracks and bridlepaths are wide enough, riders can form a double ride to enable them to chat if they wish. Horses should not, however, be paired with others which are likely to kick or bite.

It is advisable to avoid always cantering in the same areas, as anticipation may cause some horses to become fractious, and can lead to loss of ride control. If a pupil does not wish to canter, the hack escort should not insist upon it, but should allow him to bring up the rear at a steady trot instead. The rider should then remain under the responsibility of the assistant escort so as to discourage any possibility of his horse becoming upset at being left alone, or of breaking into a canter in an attempt to catch up.

General safety precautions

- Obey both the Highway Code, and the Country Code.
- Always start out at walk to establish discipline and obedience, and to allow riders the chance to settle in and become acquainted with their mount.

- Avoid obviously boggy, rutted or stony areas which may cause a horse to stumble or to go lame.
- Always give plenty of warning of changes of gait.
- Before making any upward transitions to faster gaits, always ascertain that all riders are confident to do so, and are in control.
- Where tarmac on roads is slippery, especially on downhill gradients, grass verges should be used where possible.

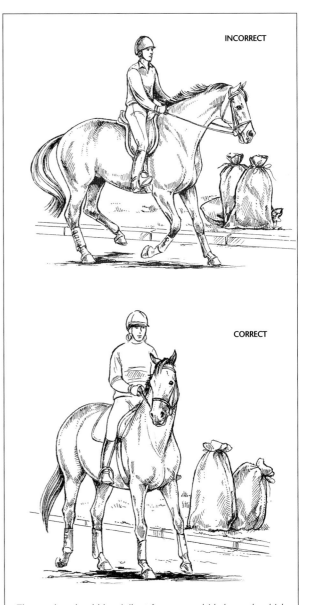

INCORRECT

CORRECT

The teacher should be vigilant for any roadside hazards which may cause a horse to shy, especially in windy conditions. The pupil should be taught how to cope in such situations or conditions before ever exposing him to them on a hack

Riding to Music

✔ The teacher must cater for all tastes: able to oblige with light-hearted chat for the 'pleasure' rider, or to be more serious for the keen student of equitation.

✔ A good teacher will be gratified by, not jealous of, his pupil's success should he ultimately become a better horseman than his mentor.

The idea of riding to music is not new, but in fact dates back hundreds of years, and today the Spanish Riding School continues the tradition with their world-famous displays. It makes an excellent teaching aid, even with pupils who are not particularly musical. Besides adding an element of fun to a lesson, it can be extremely beneficial in helping to improve regularity of rhythm, since horses as well as riders will respond to what they hear. According to the pieces chosen, it can also have profound psychological effects, being uplifting, inspiring, rousing – or conversely, soothing and relaxing if a pupil is tense or nervous.

Equipment

A good PA system is ideal, but if such a facility is unavailable, the 'ghettoblaster' type of portable audio cassette player may prove adequate provided the area in which the lesson is being conducted is not too large. Plugging the machine into the mains power, or alternatively, wiring it up to a car battery if this is possible, will be less expensive than using small internal batteries. Where a portable cassette tape player is used, it should be placed safely out of the way of the ride. Electrical equipment should not be used outdoors in wet weather.

Dust from the school can be damaging to both equipment and tapes, so if possible and safe to do so, cover them in order to minimise this. Replace tapes in their plastic cases when not in use, and use a head-cleaning cassette at regular intervals. Bright sunlight and freezing conditions can also ruin equipment, so it should all be safely stored away after the lesson; this will also reduce the likelihood of theft.

If possible, the teacher should arrange for an assistant to be available to change the music or adjust the volume, but should this not be feasible, he must be able to reach the switches himself without leaving the ride unsupervised.

Music

Cassette tapes are probably the easiest way of playing music during lessons. The teacher will find it less restrictive if he has three separate tapes with music on each appropriate to the three gaits: one tape with walk music, a second with trot music and a third with canter music; this is better than having a mixed selection on one tape because it is quicker and less troublesome to change from one tape to

another than having constantly to rewind to try and find a suitable piece of music. Provided the tapes are clearly labelled, it will also be much easier for an unmusical assistant to identify what the teacher asks for.

When selecting music, the teacher should consider the following points:

■ Vocal tracks tend to be distracting: it is best to use instrumental music.

■ Music should be chosen suitable to the pupil's age: for example, 'Nellie the Elephant' might be ideal for the very young, but an adult with more sophisticated tastes might consider it rather childish.

■ Choose music which has an appropriate rhythm and tempo for each gait.

■ Music which is familiar to pupils is helpful. There are many classical pieces suitable for riding to, but brass band and military tracks, popular pieces, contemporary instrumental music and even TV and movie themes should not be ruled out as possible sources.

Using music in lessons

Even if the horses are familiar with music being played during lessons, it should be introduced gradually, starting off at a low volume, and slowly increasing it as they become accustomed to it. The music should not be started whilst any horses are passing close to the speakers, otherwise they may be startled or frightened by it.

The teacher should check that all the pupils can hear the music, but should avoid increasing the volume to the point that his own voice cannot be heard above it. When longer discussion periods are necessary, or if a pupil asks a question, the music should either be turned down to facilitate this, or stopped completely.

Some technicalities

Certain technicalities need to be observed when playing recorded music in public – even if only for teaching. Licences in Britain should be obtained from the Performing Rights Society and from Phonographic Performance Ltd. Anyone wishing to copy recordings will also need to obtain permission from the copyright holder via a licence from the Mechanical Copyright Protection Society (see list of useful addresses on page 126).

Lectures

✔ No one person can possibly know everything.
✔ Real teaching is not 'telling' – it is about encouraging others to find out.

Giving a lecture is as much of a skill and an art as riding instruction, and its success or otherwise relies upon more than that the teacher is knowledgeable about his subject.

Lecture area

A suitable area should be available in which to give a lecture so that the teacher can ensure the minimum of disturbances, and maintain the attention of his listeners. Seating should be available, the lighting must be adequate for pupils to take notes, and the temperature comfortable. Windows will also need blinds or curtains if slides or an overhead projector is to be used to illustrate parts of the lecture.

Lectures on more practical subjects such as grooming or bandaging are best given outdoors or in a relatively spacious covered area, rather than in a stable, particularly if the group of pupils is more than two or three in number: a stable will not be large enough to accommodate more than this safely as well as the horse; also their view may be restricted.

Preparation

Whatever the theme, the lecture should have a beginning, a middle and an end. Having first introduced himself, the teacher should broadly outline the nature of the subject he intends to talk about (introduction), and its relevance and importance to his listeners; he should then move on to discuss the gist of the matter in greater depth (substance/middle section): and finish by summing up the key points covered (conclusion).

The teacher should know his subject well, having thoroughly researched it in advance. Preparatory notes may be shortened into heading form and written onto postcards, which should be clearly numbered so as to remain in correct sequence. This will act as a useful memory prompt, ensuring that the lecture progresses in a logical manner, and that vital points are not inadvertently omitted; it will also help prevent the teacher digressing from the subject, losing his train of thought, or repeating himself. These cards may be kept for future reference, adding other relevant points and updating them as necessary.

Lecture aids

Visual aids add interest to a lecture, and can be invaluable in helping pupils to understand more clearly some of the various points the teacher makes. Such aids might include the use of videos, slides, an overhead projector, posters, charts, models, and black or white boards on which headings can be written or diagrams drawn.

Any relatively complex diagram required to illustrate a point is best prepared in advance: attempting to draw it during the course of a lecture will be time-consuming, and may lead to loss of the pupils' attention whilst it is being completed.

Where lectures are of a more practical nature, the teacher should ensure that all the items he will require – such as boots, bandages, saddlery, farriery tools or feed samples – have been gathered together in readiness. If a horse is to be used as part of a demonstration, one should be selected which is of a suitable temperament, and which will not become upset or agitated by the presence of a large group.

Presentation

Good self-presentation is as important when giving a lecture as when giving a riding lesson. Teachers should avoid reading directly from notes as this tends to exclude rather than involve listeners: the action of constantly looking down may also mean that the voice does not carry well, and will not be heard clearly by those sitting further away.

The teacher should speak clearly and distinctly, adding variety to his voice by altering tone, pitch and emphasis; he should make every effort not to lapse into a monotone. He should also remember that he may need to slow his delivery slightly more than when talking normally, and he should occasionally pause briefly. Talking too fast will make it difficult for his listeners to absorb what he is saying, or to take notes if they wish.

An inexperienced teacher may find it helpful to rehearse his lecture in advance, recording it on an audio tape: replaying it later will enable him to determine how effective his delivery is, and where improvements can usefully be made. This will also help him to judge the overall length of the lecture, and to ascertain where some aspects may need to be compressed and others allotted more time, according to importance.

It is vital that the teacher can keep his pupils' interest: whilst speaking he should maintain eye contact with his listeners, not merely observe them in order to gauge whether he is holding their attention. The subject matter of some lectures may be rather dry, but the use of lecture aids, humour, and even anecdotal stories relating to the topic, may help to enliven the occasion. Another useful tactic can be for the

teacher to occasionally ask questions of his listeners: this will encourage them to think a little more for themselves, and to develop a more inquiring mind.

Handouts of notes, diagrams or suggestions for further reading about the subject may be useful to pupils, but are best passed out at the end – rather than at the beginning of, or during the lecture – in order to avoid unnecessary distraction or loss of attention. Pupils should also be discouraged from bringing food or drinks into the lecture with them, for the same reason.

Duration

The length of lectures may vary in duration, but generally speaking it may be difficult to sustain an audience's concentration for periods in excess of one hour, unless the lecture is

The use of visual aids, or displaying items relevant to the lecture topic, such as different types of bits, feed samples, or horseshoes will do much to keep the attention and interest of those listening. It can also help to clarify points the teacher wishes to make

of a practical nature, when it may successfully be more extended.

Questions

The teacher should leave time at the end of the lecture in which to answer any queries. If he is unsure of the answer to a question, he should not attempt to bluff, but should admit the fact and inquire as to whether any of the other listeners knows: and if not, research it later so he is able to give a reply during the next lecture.

PART SEVEN: Other

Considerations

Freelance Work

✔ The freelance teacher should be aware of the fact that he will need a licence from the local authority if he hires out his own horse for hacking or to teach pupils on, even if this is only on an occasional basis. It is also essential that teacher, rider and horse are insured.

Working on a freelance basis often offers greater opportunities for the teacher to instruct more serious and ambitious pupils and to tackle more challenging riding problems. He may also prefer the increase in one-to-one tuition, and probably welcome the variety and flexibility in the daily routine.

Obtaining freelance work

A freelance teacher will only gain work if he makes his existence known: advertisements may be placed in the local press, in show schedules, Riding Club and Pony Club newsletters, and on the noticeboards of saddlers, feed merchants and livery yards.

When first establishing himself as a freelance, the teacher might also consider contacting local Riding Clubs and Pony Clubs and offering his services to them free for a specified period of time, as this is a useful way of forming contacts and meeting potential clients. A set of business cards should be organised to hand out to those who express interest in using his services.

Fees

The fees charged will take into account many factors, including the teacher's experience and qualifications, travelling costs and the time it takes to reach the client, the hire of facilities if necessary (unless it has been agreed that the client arranges and pays for this separately), the length of the lesson and the number of pupils participating. The fees charged by riding schools are not usually the best guide when determining the appropriate charges, as they have considerably larger running costs and are generally able to offer a range of facilities and services beyond the scope of a freelance, and this is reflected in the price of tuition.

Drawbacks

Working as a freelance is a course of action the teacher should think through carefully before he embarks on it, as whilst the charms of such a career may be apparent, the drawbacks may be less obvious, particularly if his sole experience to date has been of riding-school work.

As a freelance, he may miss many of the advantages of a riding-school environment, including being able to ask advice from more experienced senior instructors, the

opportunity to watch others teaching and riding, a secure salary, regular set hours, days off and holidays, plus other 'perks' often offered to employees such as tuition and further training for himself, the keep of a horse, and accommodation. The facilities in which he teaches his pupils may often be more limited than those of a riding school, and earnings may be erratic due to circumstances such as lame horses, bad weather, clients going on holiday or competing at shows; in fact many freelances find it necessary to combine their teaching activities with some other part-time job in order to ensure some kind of regular and reliable income.

Teacher making an initial assessment of a new pupil

Left: A portable microphone can be a great help when teaching outdoors or anywhere the teacher's voice may not carry so well

As a freelance it will also be necessary for him to complete paperwork relating to his business: the details of his income and allowable expenses, tax returns and National Insurance contributions, and he will also have to keep his first-aid qualifications up to date; furthermore, adequate insurance cover is as essential for a freelance as it is for a riding school.

Other Roles

✔ A teacher may need to be a jack of all trades.
✔ Don't undertake a task you feel is beyond your ability.

As well as providing instruction, the teacher may also be called upon to undertake other roles for clients, either on a regular or occasional basis.

Schooling horses

A teacher may sometimes be asked to school a horse for an owner for a number of reasons: perhaps to introduce it to ridden work, to generally improve it, to help overcome some problem that the client has been having, or simply because the rider does not always have sufficient time to work it himself during the week. Suitable facilities will need to be available, appropriate insurance cover arranged, and the teacher should be sufficiently accomplished and knowledgeable a rider himself as to be able to achieve improvement and – in

(Below and right) Teachers may sometimes be asked to school horses for clients, or to prepare them for sale, but should ensure that their riding skills are sufficient for the task before accepting such requests

the case of a 'difficult' horse – to resolve problems successfully. Where schooling has been undertaken with a horse, the work done should be fully discussed with the owner, and suggestions offered as to how he can continue and build upon the progress already made. It is usually beneficial if both horse and rider can be given one or more lessons together by the teacher following a period of schooling to ensure the most satisfactory outcome for all concerned.

Training days

Local Riding and Pony Clubs organise regular training sessions and lectures for their members, and a teacher may be approached to provide instruction at these, on either a paid or voluntary basis. The teacher should satisfy himself as to insurance arrangements and the availability of a suitable venue for such occasions, as well as finding out the age and level of ability of those attending so that he can prepare himself fully beforehand and arrange for any equipment necessary to be present.

Other Roles

Examining

Teachers and proprietors of riding establishments who are involved in the training of students towards gaining recognised professional qualifications may have a particular interest in becoming examiners themselves. In order to become an ABRS or BHS examiner, an application first needs to be made to the appropriate organisation, detailing experience and qualifications currently held. Provided this meets the necessary criteria, a successful probationary period will be required before being able to become an examiner. Further details regarding working in this capacity are available by applying directly to the ABRS or BHS.

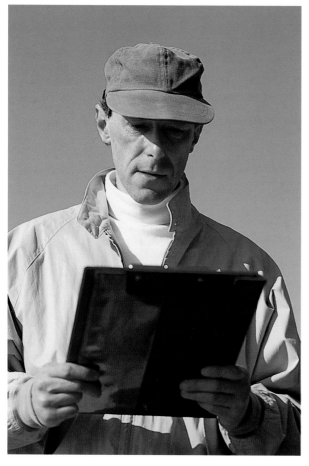

Examining can be tiring but immensely satisfying, and is one of the ways in which an interested teacher can help future generations of instructors

Assisting pupils at shows

Occasionally a pupil with his own horse may ask the teacher to accompany him to a show he is competing at. This can often give the teacher a valuable insight into problems the pupil may have encountered whilst competing previously, but which do not normally occur whilst working at home or during lessons, and can thus be a useful exercise.

Whilst working towards a competition, the teacher should strive to prepare the pupil as fully as possible, both in terms of being at the required level of ability, and in briefing him as to the rules governing the class, and procedure on the day itself. If the teacher is to call a dressage test for the pupil, this should be rehearsed once or twice at home before the day of the competition. In the case of show-jumping or cross-country classes, inexperienced pupils especially may benefit from walking the course beforehand with the teacher, who will then be able to suggest the best way of tackling it.

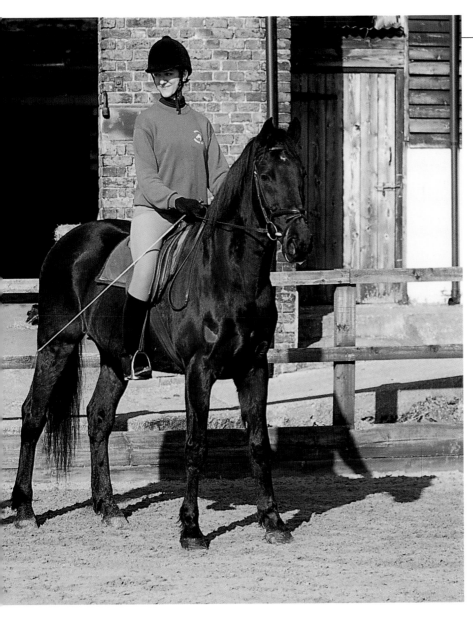

If the teacher is asked to call a test for a dressage class at a show, he should try to fit in a run through with his client during one of the pupil's lessons. This will ensure that he reads the test at a suitable speed and can be heard by the rider. In the actual test the caller would be positioned outside the arena

The teacher may also be an asset to the pupil during the warm-up phase immediately prior to a class, doing his best to impart an aura of calm and confidence and ready to help soothe any nerves. Whilst encouraging horse and pupil to produce of their best, he should remember that this is neither the time or place for a serious schooling session.

Following the competition, the teacher may wish to draw attention to any problem areas, but should attempt to do so in a positive manner and in the light of how they could be rectified in the future. He should remember to emphasise all the good points of the performance as well as the poor ones, and never indulge in sarcasm, be dismissive, or resort to abuse.

Judging at shows

Small unaffiliated shows often rely on the services of local teachers for assistance in various capacities; for example, as course builders, fence judges, secretaries, jumping, showing or dressage judges. When agreeing to take on such duties, the teacher should ascertain in advance exactly what his responsibilities will be, and at what times he will be expected to present himself, so that he may be both well prepared and punctual, and to ensure the day runs smoothly. Course plans for jumping classes should be drawn up in advance. He should be smartly and suitably dressed for the classes he is to assist with (in riding clothes if this will form part of his duties), take along any equipment he may require such as measuring sticks or tapes, and be fully conversant with the rules for all the classes he is involved in. In the case of dressage classes, if he is judging or writing for the judge, he should also know the test thoroughly.

Teachers who aspire to judging at an Affiliated level should apply to the relevant organisation for details of the discipline they are interested in.

Other Roles

Viewing of horses for sale

A pupil wishing to purchase a horse may seek advice on the matter from his teacher. If this is to be the pupil's first horse, the teacher may need to offer guidance not merely as to the height and type of horse to look for, but also be prepared to provide an honest opinion as to whether the pupil is ready for such a step. He should also ensure that the pupil is aware of the time and financial commitment involved in caring for a horse, and that he has the knowledge and practical skills necessary to cope with this, unless it is to be kept at full livery.

When accompanying a pupil to view a potential equine purchase, the teacher should remain aware that his role is that of advisor, not critic. Having viewed the horse and seen it ridden by the vendor, he should ride it himself, taking care to refrain from riding excessively hard or for an over-long period, and bearing in mind that he is assessing the animal's suitability and safety as a mount for his pupil, rather than as one for himself. He should then watch the pupil riding the horse, and although it may be helpful to offer a little advice whilst this is happening, should not develop it into a full length lesson. He should be courteous to the vendor at all times, and when discussing the horse with his client, do so privately in order to avoid giving any possible offence.

(Above and below) Politeness and courtesy should be extended at all times towards vendors, even if a horse is felt to be totally unsuitable for a client. If, in his capacity as advisor, the teacher wishes to express any unflattering views of the horse, he should do so in private

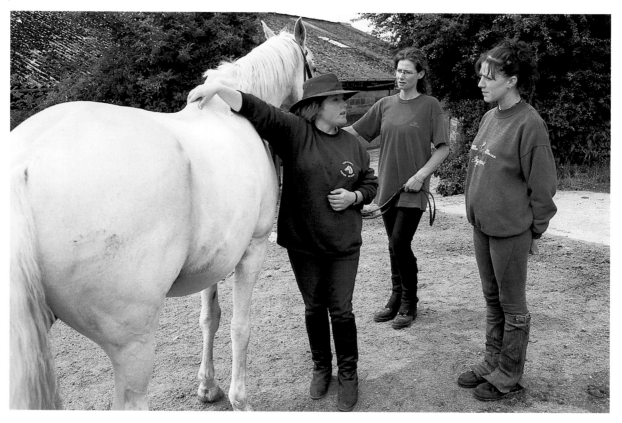

118

Course building

If a teacher is engaged to build courses for show-jumping classes, he should be well organised. He should ascertain what equipment will be available and draw up accurate course plans in advance, determining both the siting of fences and the types. Where several classes are to run consecutively in the same ring, ingenuity in the design should enable different tracks to be jumped with the minimum of alterations between each competition.

When designing courses, the teacher should attempt to set a fair test for each level and experience of horse and rider, both in terms of fence height and width, siting of fences, turns, and distances between fences. He should personally check each obstacle to make sure it has been built correctly and safely, especially if assistants – no matter how experienced – are helping to build the course. He should

If asked to assist in course building, it is helpful if the teacher can obtain some additional help with putting up fences and changing courses between classes so that lengthy delays can be avoided

also use a tape measure to check that any related distances between obstacles are appropriate for the class standard.

In his role as course builder, the teacher should also provide course plans for each class which can be posted where competitors can see it. These should include:

- the class name and/or number;
- a plan of the course, with each fence numbered appropriately and showing the direction in which each fence is to be jumped;
- the table under which the class is to be judged;
- the sequence of jump-off fences for classes where there is a second round jump-off.

Public Relations

✔ Try to make riding a positive experience, not a negative one.
✔ Patience is a virtue and a vital ingredient for a successful teacher.
✔ A smile costs nothing.

Good office organisation is essential if a riding establishment is to run smoothly, as well as to ensure the safety and wellbeing of horses and pupils, and the continued support/custom of clients. One particular person is normally responsible for one or more of these aspects, but it may be necessary on occasion for other members of staff to deputise in the event of his/her absence due, for example, to illness, or because he has been called away unexpectedly, or is on holiday. Teaching staff should therefore be familiar with the following paperwork and procedures:

- taking lesson bookings and money;
- taking lesson cancellations;
- dealing with complaints;
- making new clients welcome;
- assisting clients in filling in Client Registration Forms;
- fitting hats hired by pupils;
- taking telephone and personal enquiries;

- first aid and filling out accident/incident report forms;
- checking daily worksheets for details of lessons, and information as to hours worked by each horse;
- saddlery repair book;
- records of veterinary treatment, vaccinations, shoeing, feeding and worming of each horse kept by the establishment.

Welcoming clients

All clients, both old and new, should be made to feel welcome by staff, and that their custom is valued. If possible, new clients should be given a guided tour around the yard, when they can become familiar with its layout and the location of facilities such as toilets. They should also be invited to watch lessons in progress, and encouraged to ask any questions they may have. A good school will have nothing to hide.

(Bottom and right) Whether taking a telephone call or greeting a visitor, first impressions count, and can make the difference between gaining or losing a new client. Remember that favourable comments are one of the most effective and cheapest forms of advertising

Accident Procedure

✔ If the teacher sees that either pupil or horse are becoming fatigued, or bored with the repetition of an exercise, he should then cease that requirement, as this is when accidents are likely to occur.

The teacher is responsible for the safety of his pupils during a lesson. Whilst riding is a high risk sport and genuinely unavoidable accidents can happen, he must strive to ensure that they do not occur as a result of negligence or unsafe teaching practices. The ABRS issues guidelines on the correct completion of accident procedure, with which all teachers should be familiar, and in the event of an incident occurring at an ABRS-approved school, they should also notify the Association.

First-aid procedure

Teachers must be familiar with current first-aid procedures as detailed in the authorised manuals of St John Ambulance/St Andrew's Ambulance Association/British Red Cross, and they should also know the appropriate action to take in order to prevent further injuries arising – for instance as a consequence of a loose horse.

All teachers should have a formal first-aid qualification: these are valid for three years and must be kept up to date through further periods of training and re-examination. A member of staff who possesses a current first-aid qualification should be present at all times when trainees who do not yet have this qualification are giving lessons.

FIRST-AID FACILITIES All staff should know the whereabouts of the first-aid kit, which should be kept clean, up to date, fully stocked and never locked away but accessible at all times. Freelances should keep their own first-aid kit, and a small pocket kit should be carried by teachers escorting hacks. Suggested materials include:
- adhesive dressings (sticking plasters);
- an assortment of various sizes of sterile dressing;
- a sterile eye pad;
- two or more triangular bandages;
- crêpe bandages;
- a roll of self-adhesive tape;
- safety pins;
- scissors;
- disposable gloves;
- antiseptic solution;
- cotton wool;
- tweezers;
- blanket.

Emergency calls

All staff and trainees should be briefed on how to make telephone calls to emergency services. In situations where a telephone may not be immediately accessible – for instance, if teaching in a field some distance from the main buildings, or escorting a hack – the teacher should carry a mobile phone.

On dialling 999, give the following information whilst speaking slowly and clearly:
- which emergency service(s) is required;
- the number of the telephone you are ringing from;
- the precise location of the accident, including any road names, numbers or landmarks;
- the type and seriousness of the accident;
- the number, sex and approximate age of the casualty, plus any other information known about the nature of the injury.

The telephone receiver should not be replaced until the control officer has cleared the line.

A list of emergency numbers should be clearly displayed next to, or near to, the telephone, plus the above list detailing the information to be given when contacting them. Client records should be kept up to date, including information on who to notify in the event of an accident.

Incident Book

An incident book should be kept, both by riding schools and freelances, and entries should be written up as soon as possible following an incident. All accidents or injuries which occur should be entered, no matter how trivial they may appear at the time: also those which befall staff and trainees as well as clients, and occurring on any part of the premises, not just when specifically riding or receiving instruction.

The following details should be included in reports:
- the date on which the entry is made;
- date and time of the incident;
- full name and address of the person injured;
- name and details of any horse involved;
- name, position and qualifications of the instructor or teacher present at the time or who was first on the scene;
- location and circumstances of the incident;

- action taken, including details of the injury, treatment given, and by whom;
- whether emergency services were required;
- whether the casualty required hospital treatment;
- names of any witnesses;
- the report should be signed by the teacher, any witnesses and if possible, the person involved in the incident.

Written statements should be collected from all those concerned with, or who witnessed the incident; and if this is not possible at the time, the names and addresses noted down so they can be contacted later. Visual records should also be made, either by photograph or sketch, and any equipment involved labelled and saved.

In some instances there may also be a legal requirement to report certain types of injury or incident to the enforcing authority (see Appendix 2 Legal Requirements, page 125).

INSURANCE   All teachers should possess adequate insurance cover for public liability: freelances will need to take out their own policy, whilst employees will be covered by the riding schools' own insurance (see also Legal Requirements). It is advisable for employees as well as the self-employed to consider taking out additional personal accident insurance since they may not be covered by their Employer's Liability policy in respect of an incident which occurs outside working hours.

Should an accident happen, at no time should any admission of liability be made: the insurer should be informed of the incident as soon as possible afterwards and sent a copy of the incident report.

All teachers should be familiar with the correct course of action to take in the event of an accident

Appendices

✔ Passing an examination today doesn't mean you are a better teacher than you were yesterday or the day before – just a qualified one. Don't let it go to your head.

✔ Even after the most advanced exam has been passed, there is still ample opportunity to learn more.

✔ Qualifications simply mean you have reached a certain standard – not that you know it all.

1 THE ABRS TEACHING QUALIFICATIONS

The Association of British Riding Schools is the professional national governing body for riding school proprietors. In designing and structuring all their professional qualifications, the ABRS has sought to accommodate the career-minded person, producing for the industry the type of employee it needs, and in turn giving employers confidence in the examinations: all of them are highly practical in nature, as well as involving some degree of theory.

Each of the ABRS exams provides qualifications which are complete in themselves, i.e., they do not require the candidate to pass other supporting examinations. Each of the examinations attracts separate fees and are taken independently of each other, to make up one qualification. There is no membership fee to be paid by candidates to the Association, only a fee for the particular exam involved.

Teaching examinations are kept separate from those relating to riding and stable management, and the way they have been structured enables the examiners to fully ascertain whether each candidate has the ability and experience to assess unknown riders and horses, and to demonstrate that they can improve them within the limited time available. Great emphasis is placed upon a candidate's ability to produce, without force or aggression, and observing correct safety procedures, balanced, secure and effective riders who have an understanding of, and are in harmony with, the horses they ride. Examiners also take into consideration a candidate's ability to develop a good rapport with his pupils, and to give lessons which are both enjoyable and stimulating while taking full account of pupils' age, physique and aims; also their manner in handling customers and horses generally.

These are practical exams taken away from the candidate's normal place of work or training, and the riders used are regular riding-school clients. To ensure that candidates meet all the prerequisites for taking the examination, and stand a fair chance of success, a CV detailing training, work experience and any other qualifications held must be submitted with each application. On passing, all ABRS teaching qualification holders are registered and listed.

The ABRS Teaching Examinations range from an initial foundation qualification at one end of the scale, right up to the very highest excellence at the other. Qualifications may be eligible for funding by various bodies. Current information on this, plus full details of syllabuses, fees, examination dates, application forms, philosophy and guidance notes for each examination are available, on receipt of a large stamped, self-addressed envelop from: the Examinations Secretary, Association of British Riding Schools, Queens Chambers, Queen Street, Penzance TR18 4BH, tel: 01736 365777; exams – tel: 01736 369440; General Secretary – fax: 01736 351390; e-mail: office@abrs.org

Teaching, riding and stable management qualifications are also available from the British Horse Society (BHS). Details of these examinations can be obtained by contacting: The British Horse Society, Examinations Office, Stoneleigh Deer Park, Kenilworth, Warwickshire CV8 2XZ, tel: 01926 707700, fax: 01926 707800, e-mail: enquiry@bhs.org.uk

GRADING OF TEACHERS

Any person placed in sole charge of a lesson or hack should be suitably qualified to do so, both in terms of formal qualifications and/or relevant experience. Before being asked to undertake any instruction of riding-school clientele for commercial purposes, students working towards obtaining their first teaching qualification should participate in teaching practice training sessions to ensure that correct and safe teaching practices are understood and observed. All such sessions, and any commercial tuition given by unqualified students, should be supervised at all times by a qualified member of staff.

Levels of competence

Qualified teachers should be capable of providing private and group tuition to the following levels, whilst observing correct safety procedures at all times:

1 Holders of the initial foundation ABRS teaching qualification should be able to teach basic levels in a riding school without supervision, including:

- working gaits in walk, trot and canter;
- work without stirrups in walk, trot and canter;
- riding school figures accurately, eg circles, serpentine loops, changes of rein;
- drill rides;
- simple polework exercises and knowledge of distances to set between poles;
- show-jumping tuition over single fences, and short courses over varied obstacles up to a height of 2ft 6in (76cm); also a knowledge of the distances for one-stride doubles.

2 In addition to teaching the above with increased depth of knowledge, more experienced ABRS teachers holding the next level of qualification will also be able to provide sound instruction on the following:
- riding with two pairs of reins;
- gait variants;
- preparing the horse for lateral movements;
- turn on the forehand;
- introduction to counter canter;

- shoulder-in;
- show-jumping and cross-country tuition over single fences and courses, and also simple gymnastic jumping exercises, over a variety of obstacles up to a height of 3ft (91cm); this including knowledge of related distances between fences;
- lunge lessons to improve rider posture;
- leading and escorting hacks.

3 Holders of the very highest level of ABRS teaching qualification will be able to teach to an advanced level, including:
- advanced lateral work: shoulder-in, travers, renvers, half pass, counter canter, single flying changes, rein back, pirouettes;
- lunge work to improve the horse's way of going, as well as lunge lessons to improve rider posture;
- show-jumping and cross-country tuition over single fences and courses, and gymnastic jumping exercises over obstacles of 3ft 6in (107cm) and above.

2 LEGAL REQUIREMENTS

There are certain legal requirements and obligations which managers and proprietors of riding schools should be aware of, and must comply with. These include:

- The Riding Establishments Acts 1964 and 1970
- Animals Act 1971
- Public Liability Insurance
- Occupiers Liability Acts 1957 and 1984
- Employers Liability (Compulsory Insurance) Act 1969
- Health & Safety at Work Act 1974
- Fire Precautions Act 1971 (where hostel accommodation is provided)
- Employment Protection Consolidation Act 1978

- COSHH Regulations 1988
- Guidance Regulations of July 1990 relevant to the Health & Safety (First Aid) Regulations of 1981
- The Reporting of Injuries, Diseases and Dangerous Occurences Regulations (RIDDOR) 1985
- Employers must also keep adequate records of employees' wages, deductions of PAYE tax and National Insurance contributions, and pay such tax and National Insurance contributions as they become due.
- National Minimum Wage 1998
- European Working Time Directive 1998
- Fairness at Work Bill 1999
- Welfare of Animals (Transport) Order 1997

Useful Reading and Addresses

Reading

At the time of going to press, the following publications are all available from the ABRS office in Penzance (see below).

Guidelines for ABRS Tests Equitation & Stable Management (ABRS)

Harris, Charles, FIH FABRS FBHS *Fundamentals of Riding*

Initial Teaching Award Guidelines & Skills Check Workbook (ABRS)

Renowden, Shirley, FABRS *Drills & Formation Riding*

Silverman, Tony *An Instructor's Pocket Guide to Safe and Interesting Hacking*

Addresses

Association of British Riding Schools (ABRS)
38–40 Queens Chambers, Queen Street, Penzance, Cornwall TR18 4BH

British Dressage
National Agricultural Centre, Stoneleigh Park, Kenilworth, Warwickshire CV8 2RJ

British Horse Society (BHS)
Stoneleigh Deer Park, Kenilworth, Warwickshire CV8 2XZ

British Eventing
Stoneleigh Park, Kenilworth, Warwickshire CV8 2RN

British Show Jumping Association (BSJA)
Stoneleigh Park, Kenilworth, Warwickshire CV8 2LR

Mechanical Copyright Protection Society
Elgar House, 41 Streatham High Road, London SW16 1ER

The Performing Rights Society
29–23 Berners Street, London W1P 4AA

Phonographic Performance Ltd
Ganton House, 14–22 Ganton Street, London W1V 1LB

The Pony Club
NAC Stoneleigh Park, Kenilworth, Warwickshire CV8 2RW

Riding for the Disabled Association
Avenue R, National Agricultural Centre, Kenilworth, Warwickshire CV8 2LY

Side Saddle Association
Highbury House, 19 High Street, Welford, Northamptonshire NN6 6HT

Photography credits

Photographs on pp35(top rt, ctr rt, btm rt), 58–61 copyright © Kit Houghton
Photographs on pages 47 and 107 copyright © Bob Langrish

The publishers wish to thank Suzanne's Riding School for providing the excellent location, riders and horses for the photography in this book.

Index